MOMOLOGY

A MOM'S GUIDE TO SHAPING GREAT KIDS

SHELLY RADIC

Revell

a division of Baker Publishing Group
Grand Rapids, Michigan

© 2010 by MOPS International

Published by Revell
a division of Baker Publishing Group
P.O. Box 6287, Grand Rapids, MI 49516-6287
www.revellbooks.com

Printed in the United States of America

Library of Congress Cataloging-in-Publication Data

Radic, Shelly
    Momology : a mom's guide to shaping great kids / Shelly Radic.
       p.   cm.
    Includes bibliographical references.
    ISBN 978-0-8007-3449-7 (pbk.)
       1. Mother and child—Religious aspects—Christianity. 2. Motherhood—Religious aspects—Christianity. 3. Child rearing—Religious aspects—Christianity. 4. Parenting—Religious aspects—Christianity. I. Title.
    BV4529.18.R33 2010
    248.8'45—dc22   2010003582

10   11   12   13   14   15   16   7   6   5   4   3   2   1

To every mom
Godspeed as you shape the future

CONTENTS

FOREWORD

Naomi Cramer Overton,
President, MOPS International

I wish I had access to *Momology: A Mom's Guide to Shaping Great Kids* when my children were younger! In *Momology*, Shelly Radic has articulated what I knew in my gut to be true—that mothering is an inexact process of figuring out what works for me and my family, and that while there are foundational principles, each child will stretch and challenge our mothering expertise in different ways.

As president of MOPS International, I have many opportunities to listen to moms from around the country and around the world—moms like you. And what I hear from you is that regardless of your circumstances, you want to be the best mom for your child. What's new is that you don't want to just accept what "experts" say about how you should do mothering. You want to be equipped to discern your own mothering style. This book represents voices of moms from different backgrounds, perspectives, and even places on their spiritual journeys. It combines those voices with research on areas that are essential to shaping our children. The research confirmed four key areas to effective mothering—a healthy, resilient mom; understanding of basic parenting skills; supportive relationships; and a spiritual foundation.

In my own experience, I found a community of moms who accepted me and encouraged me during a season of mothering when I felt overwhelmed by the needs of three young children. I was especially stretched by some unexpected needs that came with my youngest child. At that point in my life, I know I wanted to shape great kids, but many of the parenting theories that were clear to me before motherhood didn't seem to apply in my situation. In my MOPS community I found women who loved me and loved my children. They encouraged me to discover how to be a mom while still being Naomi. They celebrated with me in the good times and supported me in the hard times. This left me renewed in mind, body, soul, and spirit so I could become a better mom and a better me.

That's why I'm excited about *Momology* and the framework that Shelly has provided for moms of young children. Shelly and her husband have impressed me as lifelong learners in their parenting. In addition, Shelly's living faith in Jesus comes through in these pages. While you will be encouraged by stories from Shelly's rich experience as a mom of four, you will also hear from many other moms, and be guided through foundational mothering principles in an engaging and thought-provoking way. All this is for the purpose of providing *you* as a mom with essential tools for your own growth as you are shaping your children.

Momology is more than a book. It is also an open, accepting community of moms where you can share ideas, process experiences, and learn together. None of us are meant to mother alone. Relationships in a mothering community are essential for equipping you to be the best mom for your child. While we are focused on shaping our children during the intense early mothering years, we are also being shaped as women and as mothers. Much of this positive interaction occurs in community with other moms.

I hope you can share this book and the accompanying web resources with all your mom friends, so they too can shape great kids. Don't just read this book; share it with others and consider together how you can be better moms and make a better world.

Naomi

INTRODUCTION

I watched with interest as mothers stuffed their small children into coats and mittens in preparation for an icy-cold trek to the car. One particular mom-daughter-baby trio caught my attention. The daughter, somewhere between two and three, stood over a jacket with its arms stretched out on the floor in front of her, hood almost between her feet. Suddenly she swooped down, pushed her arms into the sleeves, and attempted to swing the jacket over her head and onto her body. Caught on her knit cap, the jacket failed to go on. After shrugging back out of the sleeves, the little girl looked to her mom. Bouncing the bundled baby, her mom simply said, "Try again" and the little girl did. No success, the jacket caught on the cap again. Her mom responded, "What else could you try?" The little girl thought for a moment before her eyes lit up and she yanked off the cap and threw it to the ground. Arranging the jacket once again, she swooped down for another try. The jacket sailed over her head and slid in place down her back, the hood gently framing her face. Her victorious grin mirrored her mom's.

I admired the little girl's patience and creativity, but I admired her mom even more. Instead of hurrying through the snow clothes routine, she encouraged her daughter to try a creative solution, even when it meant trying and failing and trying again.

For just about my entire life, I've been fascinated by how moms do this mom thing. As a girl, I remember watching new moms, wrinkled and bent moms, and moms surrounded with hordes of kids as they received prizes every Mother's Day for having tiny babies, for being moms for a long, long time, and for getting the most kids to sit together in church at one time. I also watched my own pretty amazing mom juggle husband, kids, home, job, friendships, and volunteer work with ease (she's since confessed it wasn't as easy as she made it look).

Just before I had my first child, I smugly watched moms, quite certain I would manage with ease where they struggled to succeed. I had my list of "I will nevers," "my children will nevers," and "nevers in a million years." During my first couple years as a mom, I didn't do much watching, certain I had the mom thing down pretty well. At about the two-year point, I started watching again, my list of nevers quickly disintegrating (bet you can guess why!) to be replaced by a longer list of "another mom does this better," "her kids do that better," and "I better get better or my child is doomed." For a while, mom watching became a distressing spectator sport in which my home team rarely came out on top.

Four children and two decades of mothering and mom watching later, I'm comfortable enough in my own momness to once again appreciate and learn from other moms. Working in an organization that provides opportunities for moms to connect with other moms, I'm convinced that moms are impressive. As I watch moms, I'm more certain than ever that as we fulfill the all-important role of shaping our children and the world in which they grow up, we are the most creative, resourceful people on the planet. We have to be—the future of the planet snuggles up at our sides, plays at our feet, looks to us for love and direction.

Moms are artists, combining ideas and resources in personalized, creative ways. We are also scientists, testing a hypothesis we think will work for us as mothers. We tweak it again and again until the creative and scientific processes merge into something that works for us and our kids—a way to mother that is uniquely our own.

Momology: A Mom's Guide to Shaping Great Kids is based on research and mom-creativity. We learned from research done by organizations including Search Institute, the YMCA, and Barna as well as parenting experts, government agencies, and major universities. Just as important, we learned from surveys of moms like you. About 1,800 moms participated in surveys conducted for *Momology*; still others shared their stories and ideas during one-on-one interviews. *Momology* was shaped by a team of moms—veterans and rookies. What we learned together influenced the selection of four areas we believe contribute to shaping great kids.

- Knowing who we are: building a healthy, resilient mom CORE
- Knowing what we're capable of: developing FINESSE in the ways we daily interact with our kids
- Knowing who we can count on: interacting within a CIRCLE of relationships that support us and our kids
- Knowing who God is: engaging with him in his GRAND-SCAPE

These areas are covered in four separate sections, each divided into short, naptime-sized bites that include stories from an assortment of moms (Field Study), survey results (Mom Stats and Voices   Mom Stats   **VOICES**), research information (with source information given in endnotes), and my own experiences as a mom. There's also a place for your thoughts (Practicum).

Although you can explore each section on your own, I encourage you to do it in community. Discuss Practicums with a friend, mentor, or your mom group. Whenever you see this symbol [M] , share with other moms online at mom-ology.org.

Motherhood is a huge responsibility, one that's more easily accomplished in community. We learn from each other's creative approaches, from both failed and successful attempts to be better moms. Together we can explore this enormous mom-job from multiple angles and perspectives, allowing what we learn to guide us in shaping great kids.

Between Me, Myself, and I

Me: She's been crying all night. What's bothering her?

Myself: Maybe I'm just not cut out to be a mom.

I: Sometimes she likes it when I rub her back. I'll try that next.

Me: She's still crying. And she just spit up all down my back. Yuck! What next?

Myself: I'm such a loser. Everything I try just makes things worse.

I: I'll put her right next to my skin. She liked that last night and I can take off this smelly shirt.

Me: She's starting to calm down. Will she actually fall asleep?

Myself: The second I lay her back in the crib, she'll start screaming again. I'll probably be holding her forever.

I: I think it's working. Maybe I'm getting this middle of the night mom thing figured out.

Me: Is she sleeping yet? Can I put her down?

PART ONE

CORE

core (noun): the central, innermost, or most essential part of anything

core (noun): a mom's unique, inner self, including her temperament, life experiences, emotions, passions, and potential

Core Resilience

"Pat it, and roll it, and mark it with a B. Then put it in the oven for baby and me." Singing these words to my daughter, the voice I heard sounded strangely like the voice of . . . my mother! What? Where did that come from? Like the B on the baker's cake, my mothering was marked by her mothering.

Even before we're born, our reactions to all the new experiences and responsibilities of mothering are being shaped. Those reactions come from our inner core, which begins forming the moment of conception, when cells divide and mama chromosomes pair up with daddy chromosomes in a unique pattern. Our inner core continues developing through childhood and our pre-mom adult years. After we become mothers, we respond to all the newness of motherhood from that core, that unique inner self that includes temperament, life experiences, emotions, passions, and potential. Our core shapes the way we shape our children, and moms with a strong, resilient core are more likely to shape strong, resilient children.

Sit ups and leg lifts—even those beloved Kegel exercises—develop strong core muscles, the ones in our tummy, back, and hips. These core muscles need to be well-developed to make our bodies more resilient to the physical activities we encounter each day. Likewise, a strong inner core needs to be well-developed to make our lives more resilient to all the new stuff that comes our way as moms.

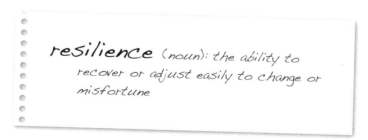

resilience (noun): the ability to recover or adjust easily to change or misfortune

Why is resilience so important to children? Why is your resilience so important to them? It turns out that resilience has been identified as one of the five protective factors *known* to reduce the risk of child abuse and neglect.[1]

According to the U.S. Department of Health and Human Services (HHS), resilient parents and children are likely to feel that

1. they are important and valuable to someone who cares for and about them;
2. life is basically good even when bad things happen;
3. there is meaning to life that is bigger and greater than "me" and "now."

If we moms can deliver those three items to our children, we're well on our way to shaping great kids. But resilience doesn't help just children. It helps moms. HHS defines parental resilience this way:

> Resilience is the ability to handle everyday stressors and recover from occasional crises. Parents who are emotionally resilient have a positive attitude, creatively problem solve, effectively address challenges, and are less likely to direct anger and frustration at their children. In addition, these parents are aware of their own challenges—for example, those arising from inappropriate parenting they received as children—and accept help and/or counseling when needed.[2]

So, our first unit of study in momology? A look at mom resilience.

FIELD STUDY

To the Heart

We moved frequently during my childhood and both my parents worked, so I learned at an early age to dig in and figure out how to make things happen in new situations. I also developed a knack for making friends in new places. My dad was a pastor, and he pushed me to take leadership in a variety of situations. He also encouraged my natural optimism as he modeled trust in God during good times and bad.

When my son Jacob was born, I didn't realize he had a life-threatening heart defect until we were sent straight to the hospital from a two-week checkup. Sitting in the hospital, my postpartum emotions wildly fluctuating and my lactating breasts leaking all over my shirt, I learned Jake was lucky to be alive and needed immediate angioplasty to have any hope of staying that way.

Jacob's initial surgery spared his life, but he would need close monitoring and several more surgeries on his little heart. As he recovered from the first surgery, I was overwhelmed, scared, and angry, especially angry at God. I had been doing the hard work of mothering four stepsons, really investing in those boys, and I thought God should've honored all my hard work as a stepmom by giving me a healthy baby of my own.

Soon, though, my innate optimism and determination to dig in and figure things out kicked in. I dug deeper into my childhood faith and discovered I could trust God with Jacob's situation. I got to know Jake's medical team, a great group of people who cared about Jacob and me. I researched Jacob's condition, learning as much as I could about his special needs.

At home, I protected my boy like a mama bear, keeping away the germs and monitoring his activities closely, sometimes too closely. When Jacob was older, his heart specialist had to talk me into letting him do normal boy things, like crossing the street by himself!

When Jacob turned ten, he had open-heart surgery that corrected his condition and allowed him to lead a healthy, active life. By that time, I was involved in supporting other moms of children with serious heart conditions and even started a foundation to raise money for pediatric heart health care.

—Bonnie, mom of six

Mom Stats

Being a mom has made me . . .

More resilient: 93.9%
Less resilient: 6.1%

Mom Stats

When my life changes, I . . .

Go with the flow: 15.5%
Quickly work to make needed
   adjustments: 33.5%
First work at staying calm, then make
   needed adjustments: 27.3%
Usually feel stuck for a while before
   making adjustments: 20.6%
Have a difficult time moving
   forward: 3.1%

Can you discern how the resilience Bonnie needed to handle a challenging period in her early mothering experience was shaped? You probably noted she's an optimist, had to figure out new situations at an early age, learned to build relationships quickly, and had parents who modeled faith at work. Just as Bonnie's temperament and life experiences influenced how she mothered Jake, so your core will influence the way you mother.

From her resilient core, a mom finds the following:

- Strength to deal with mom challenges
- Discernment for making parenting decisions
- Self-control to manage responses and behaviors
- Humility to ask for help when needed
- Self-regard to do something she loves at least once a week
- Flexibility to deal with change
- Gratitude to express thanksgiving and appreciation
- Adaptability to manage conflict and stress
- Determination to utilize her influence
- Authenticity to create sustainable community
- Integrity to live out what she believes is important

 Practicum

* Has being a mom made me more or less resilient?
* Since becoming a mom, I've had to dig deep within myself in order to . . .

4 Exercises for Building Resilience

1. Incorporate at least one stress management technique—such as exercise, listening to relaxing music, or journaling—into your daily life.
2. Make a plan for crises before you need one. What life circumstances do you fear most? Create a list of resources to use if this happens.
3. Reduce stressors. Make a list of things that regularly cause stress in your life. Select one and find a way to reduce its impact.
4. Learn to ask for help, for answers, for advice. Write down what needs to be said and practice saying it in front of your mirror. Learn to ask yourself: what do I truly need?

1.1 Getting to Know Me

1.1.1 Temperament

Mothering is a crash course in self-discovery. I adored my daughter—holding, feeding, and comforting her were amazing experiences—but I struggled to find new ways to be me. During early mothering, even our self-talk is filled with questions. *Where did that latent ability to organize tiny little onesies and socks come from? How come I get so frustrated by the myriad of opinions on feeding babies? How did I attune so quickly to my baby's different cries? Why do I spend hours researching day-care providers even when I feel comfortable with my current option?* Temperament, determined by the genes we inherited, influences the answer to many of those questions.

Introvert or extrovert? People- or task-oriented? Practical or abstract thinker? Right from the start we're wired with a certain temperament, a distinct nature and character foundational to our core. As we watch our children, we often notice clues to their temperament at an early age. One infant enjoys being with a large group of people, another thrives with one-on-one attention. One toddler is in perpetual motion, another is happiest sitting on mom's lap with a lift-the-flap book. One preschooler studies a playground situation carefully before participating, another jumps in without a thought. I once heard temperament referred to as the lenses through which we view all of life. Some of us have blue lenses; some have yellow; some have red. How can knowing your temperament shape great kids?

We accept who we are, the choices we make, and the ways we react. One mom's need for alone time, away from her child, makes sense when she knows, as an introvert, she'll be better able to process life because of that time away.

We understand how and why we react to others. Feeling impatient when a friend spends hours researching the best brand of diapers instead of grabbing the sale brand like we do is easier to understand when we realize we're simply wired differently!

We realize how our personality impacts those around us, especially our children. A spontaneous mom can consider ways to tailor her approach to life to include a child who thrives on carefully considered plans and well-ordered routines.

In her book *A Woman's Guide to Personality Types*, author Donna Partow provides another way to understand our temperaments.[3] Based on the DiSC behaviorial profile, Partow identifies four different personality types. Below is a quick summary of the primary traits and response patterns for each type.

Director—wants control
- Traits—driven by an active will and the need to get results
- Under pressure—responds through outbursts
- From others—needs respect and the acceptance of their ideas

Cheerleader—has fun, wants to be loved
- Traits—driven by emotion and the need to influence
- Under pressure—responds with intense emotion and talking
- From others—seeks approval, camaraderie, attention

Investigator—brings perfection
- Traits—driven by logic and the need to do things right
- Under pressure—responds by withdrawing and thinking negatively
- From others—wants assurance and recognition for competency

Mentor—takes life easy, lives in peace
- Traits—driven by a passive will and the need to help
- Under pressure—responds by withdrawing and becoming fatigued
- From others—wants sincere appreciation and harmony

Knowing our temperament allows us to identify and work within areas of strengths, and identify and reduce the impact of weaknesses. For instance, Bonnie's temperament allowed her to quickly build relationships with Jacob's caregivers—a strength. Her tendency to be controlling led her to be overprotective—a weakness.

Practicum

* Consider taking a free online temperament assessment at
  www.humanmetrics.com/cgi-win/JTypes2.asp. Based on
  Myers-Briggs research, this assessment can help you better
  understand how you view life and respond to situations.
  (Please note: We've used the personality tool successfully
  here at MOPS, but be aware that there are many other assessments available on the site that MOPS does not use or
  recommend.)

* How is your temperament shaping the way you mother?

* Ask a friend to identify your type. Do the same for her.

* Discuss how you see each other compared to how you see
  yourselves.

1.1.2 Life Experiences

My friend Alexandra, an only child who was raised by her
single mom, offers a glimpse into how life experiences shape us,
how our past experiences impact our core.

For Alex, much of her childhood was spent traveling. Her mom,
an ESL (English as a Second Language) teacher, was on the move
to see the next corner of the world. Where she went, Alex went.
She remembers eating squid in Barcelona, visiting wineries in Italy,
and going to the pyramids outside Mexico City. By the fourth
grade, she had gone to five different schools in two countries.
She knew life looked, sounded, smelled, and tasted different in
different places.

But her experiences weren't all positive. Constantly moving, Alex didn't always know where she fit in the world. As an only child with an absent father and no living grandparents, she felt her roots did not go deep. There was often a yearning for a larger family or community with a shared history.

Then she met and married Derek, who grew up on the same piece of property that his mother did—three generations raised in one place. She saw the benefits of a large extended family and Derek's strong sense of roots and his place in the world. Dreaming about her future, Alex wanted her children to experience a hybrid of both their family models: she wanted to expose her kids to God's broad world within the context of a more traditional (and probably stationary) family.

Alex, now a mother of three girls, has both embraced and reshaped her experiences into what she is offering her own children. She and Derek have made many intentional decisions about where they live, work, and go to school that expose their family to the larger world through everyday interactions and yet provide a sense of stability for their children.

Dear Abby once offered these wise words on the power of past experience to shape current life: "Don't let your past dictate who you are, but let it be a part of who you will become." Dear Abby had it right. While our past is part of who we become, it does not have to dictate who we are or how we mother.

Like Alex, we each enter motherhood with a mixed bag of life experiences that need to be embraced and reshaped into the experience we offer our children. Life experience

Mom Stats

In considering their life experiences,

- 83.5% of moms said they felt loved, safe, and well cared for as children
- 16.5% of mothers did not

includes such things as culture, environment, upbringing, and education.

VOICES

The part of my childhood that most shapes my mothering is . . .

The absolute safety I felt at all times.

—Jen, mom of six

My mom let us build forts in the living room and keep them there for days and was just a "go with the flow" kind of mother.

—Susie, mom of three

How to channel anger. My mom used to be quiet for three days, when I was young. I hated that. I think it's better to talk it out and be done with it.

—Beth, mom of one

Being encouraged to "find things to do" on my own—I had to use my imagination to stay busy and it has helped me become a laid-back and flexible person.

—Laura-Jean, mom of three

> Losing my mom at age eleven made me realize that we need to make the most of our time since we don't know when our time of influence will be over.
>
> —Kathie, mom of three

Whichever category you fall into, the story of your life experiences will impact your mothering. However, you are responsible for shaping the experiences of your own family. As we sort through who we are and who we want to be as moms, it often helps to spend time considering our life experiences, either individually or with a trusted friend, mentor, or counselor. Which experiences make raising your children easier? Which make it harder? How you respond to and change because of life experiences determines the strength of your core resilience.

 Practicum

* As a child, my physical needs (safety, health care, food, shelter), emotional needs, and higher-level needs (like respect, confidence, and space for creative thinking) were met (or not met) by . . .
* This influences the way I mother when . . .
* The parts of my life experience I want to pass on to my child are . . .
* The parts of my life experience I want to reshape include . . .

If your life experiences include especially challenging issues such as abuse, abandonment, mental illness, profound loss, or substance abuse, time with a trained counselor may provide the best support. Friends, colleagues, church staff, medical professionals, insurance providers, or local health agencies are good sources for referrals.

1.1.3 Powerful Emotions

"How dare you touch my son!" The young mom was shocked and embarrassed by her reaction to a store clerk who was gently redirecting her preschooler away from the broken escalator. Where did that sudden panic over a stranger come from? She wondered if it was a response to the fear she felt as a child after a neighbor friend was abducted. As we encounter the new experiences of mothering, powerful emotions often surface. Some of them, such as happiness, joy, and acceptance, are positive and contribute to a strong core. Other emotions such as guilt, sadness, bitterness, and anger have the ability to undermine our resilience. These negative emotions, if allowed free reign, can wreak havoc with the positive environment we desire for our children.

Everyone has broken and wounded places that may carry with them powerful negative emotions. Some of the broken and wounded places have been imposed on us, others have been self-inflicted. What do we do with the memories of jealously taunting a sibling, or being subjected to teasing about a speech impediment, or of a belittling litany of "you're so stupid, you never do anything right"?

For that matter, what do we do with difficult emotions stemming from experiences occurring right now as we mother? How do we handle the shame that occurs while waiting in line at a food bank after a job loss or the guilt over letting a toddler stay in the playpen a while longer because we're tired of cleaning up messes? What about the anger and frustration that lashes out at family members in the midst of cooking dinner because we are exhausted by the incessant demands of a long day? The following three steps have helped me work through some of my own negative emotions.

- **Assess:** What experience may be causing my negative emotions (like guilt, shame, resentment, or anger)?
- **Assign:** Who owns responsibility for the experience? (Sometimes it helps to designate percentages!)
- **Address:** How will I take ownership for my emotional healing?

Let's apply these three steps to the story below. Sometimes it's helpful to work through someone else's emotions before we tackle our own.

Tamrae's mom and stepdad worked until six every night. As a young teen, Tamrae was responsible for watching three younger siblings and making dinner. One evening, after putting some water on to boil for pasta, Tamrae went into the family room to settle a squabble between two of her siblings. While she was out of the kitchen, her three-year-old sister, Tessa, decided to stir the pot and in doing so, was badly scalded. Tessa was left with ugly, permanent scars. As Tamrae expected, her stepdad blamed her for the incident, calling her careless, irresponsible, stupid, and cruel. The incident happened long ago, but with her own daughter now beside her in the kitchen, those shaming words are a continuous loop of guilt and fear running through Tamrae's mind.

- Assess: What experience is causing Tamrae's negative emotions? (Possible answer: Her sister's accident that occurred while she was babysitting.)
- Assign: Who owns responsibility for the experience? (Possible answers: Tamrae, squabbling siblings, mom and stepdad who left her with too much responsibility.)
- Address: How can Tamrae take ownership for her own healing? (Possible answers: forgive herself; talk to her sister about the experience.)

 Practicum

* The emotions I see most in my own mothering are . . .
* I can tell these emotions make my children . . .
* Take some time to assess, assign, and address any negative emotions currently impacting your core.
* Share about ways you are dealing with emotions at mom-ology.org. [M]

1.1.4 The Art of Forgiveness

When my oldest daughter, Brittany, was three, my family met an incredible four-year-old girl in need of a family. As soon as we were licensed, she joined us as a foster/adopt placement. A year into the process, there was a social worker change. The new social worker did not think we were a good match racially and began working to move our foster daughter to another family.

Although we went through many channels to continue adoption proceedings, after five months the little girl was moved to live with a relative. Although this eventually had the wonderful outcome of reunification with her birth mother, my husband, Brittany, and I were deeply hurt. I found myself struggling to forgive two people—the social worker and myself. I experienced great guilt for putting Brittany through such a traumatic loss, for breaking my promise of a "forever sister."

For me, the social worker was the easiest to forgive. Not easy mind you, but easier than forgiving myself for inflicting emotional pain and breaking a promise to my daughter. As a matter of fact, the need to forgive myself still crops up from time to time, usually when Britt is struggling with relationships, her fear of losing someone she cares about once again doing battle with her need for friendship. My shame will start spreading like a big black splotch across my thinking, needing to be erased before it takes over my core. Experience has taught me that this shameful self-talk is unhealthy and forgiving myself needs to be addressed quickly. I find these words, penned by Lewis B. Smedes, both comforting and motivating:

> Forgiving is a journey, sometimes a long one. We may need some time before we get to the station of complete healing, but the nice thing is that we are being healed en route. When we genuinely forgive, we set a prisoner free and then discover the prisoner we set free was us.[4]

As we get to know ourselves, we usually encounter things we wish were not a part of our story, things placed there by choice as well as hard stuff we didn't choose. Forgiving ourselves and others can be a challenging, time-consuming process. But the benefits are enormously important for shaping and maintaining a resilient mom core. Medical research shows that forgiveness offers many benefits, including

- Lower blood pressure
- Stress reduction
- Better anger management skills
- Lower risk of substance abuse
- Fewer symptoms of depression and anxiety
- More friendships
- Healthier friendships
- Greater spiritual well-being [5]

On the flip side, when we don't forgive, both moms and children suffer, opening the door to angry outbursts, grudges that destroy a sense of belonging and community, self-talk contaminated by revenge, and a low sense of self-worth.

FIELD STUDY

Forgiveness— It's Worth It

I expected toes to be stepped on when I clicked "publish post" on that blog entry. I knew it was a divisive topic, and I had weighed the risk of being authentic. What I didn't expect was for it to cause a crisis among my friends.

Within minutes of posting, emails flew with accusations and frustrations. Instant messages shot across the internet like bullets. What started as an attempt at authenticity degraded into misunderstanding, anger, and gossip. One friend, upset by what she had read, went to another friend who became upset by what she heard. Both sent me their reactions of how they felt.

I felt attacked and misunderstood. They felt angry and hurt. To call it a crisis is an understatement; it was a personal cataclysm. My entire girlfriend ecosystem was imploding. I spent that long night pouring over each word I'd written and trying to see how they could have possibly misunderstood it. I mentally rehearsed what I could say to defend myself and rehashed what they'd said that had hurt me. That night was the first time since junior high that I cried myself to sleep because of girlfriend trouble.

After a soggy sleep, I considered my options. I could:

1. Attempt to avoid further pain by avoiding the people involved. (Kind of hard to do when they are your best friends and you love them.)
2. Build up my own contingent of "defenders" and see which side would win (a war I was old enough to know that no one would win).
3. Do the hard work of honestly addressing each hurt and trying to work through them, apologizing for what needed forgiving, and forgiving what needed to be forgiven.

I went with option three because I knew it was the right thing to do and because I knew I desperately needed that girlfriend ecosystem to keep me alive and growing as a mom and a woman. It was messy and painful and required risk.

> We didn't do it "right" or even "well." There were tears and angry words. There was that first face-to-face meeting that made me nervous and nauseous. There were lessons learned and remembered. Eventually? There were shared smiles, then giggles and laughs and new memories.
>
> —Tracey, mom of three

How can we forgive ourselves and others?

- Look again at the benefits of forgiveness listed on page 32. Then look at what happens when we don't forgive. What do you really want?
- What specific offense do you need to forgive?
- When appropriate, gently share the offense with the other person involved.
- If sharing is inappropriate, impossible, or you need to forgive yourself, write out the offense.
- Choose to forgive. Let go of bitterness, anger, resentment, and thoughts of revenge.
- Consider using a symbolic act to signify forgiveness has taken place. Share a meal together, shake hands, or shred and discard the paper holding the offense.
- Invite God to be part of the forgiveness, providing wisdom, direction, and continued healing. He's very experienced.

Be gentle with one another, sensitive. Forgive one another as quickly and thoroughly as God in Christ forgave you.

—Ephesians 4:32 Message

Forgive yourself and others. Everyone makes mistakes. Forgiving those mistakes prevents long-term damage to your core and is beneficial for shaping resilient moms and kids.

 Practicum

* My biggest barrier to forgiveness is . . .
* My own experiences with forgiveness have taught me . . .
* I need to forgive . . .
* Share what you are learning about forgiveness at mom-ology.org. Ⓜ

1.1.5 Depression

Things like splashing through rainy day puddles in yellow rubber boots dance through our daydreams about motherhood. Happiness, contentment, joy—aren't those the emotions most often associated with mothers? That we might be part of the 20 to 25 percent of women who experience depression isn't something we dream, or even want to think about. Yet depression has been called the most significant mental health risk for women, especially women of childbearing and childrearing age.[6] Postpartum depression (PPD), PMS, perimenopause, winter depression, and biochemical imbalances are some of the most common forms of depression mothers experience.

It's scary to think about depression. It should be—the overwhelming sadness, feelings of worthlessness, and disconnect from everyday life aren't healthy for mother or child. But moms can and do recover. What do moms and families who've recovered from depression look like? After clicking through the Surviving and Thriving online photo album,[7] two answers come to mind: happy and normal. Viewing these happy, normal-looking families is a bright spot in the field of women's depression. Depression can be treated.

Receiving treatment as early as possible is important, so it's critical for moms to be aware of depression symptoms and how to seek help. The longer depression is left untreated, the more likely it is that her child will experience some form of depression.[8]

Dr. Carrie Carter—pediatrician, mother, and depression survivor—describes seeking treatment like this:

> When in that dark, isolated place, each of us needs someone to toss down a "rope" to help pull us out. That "rope" or treatment may come in the form of support from loved ones, the help of a counselor or mental health treatment with medications by a psychiatrist—or all the above! Your job is to let others know you need help and then grab onto the "rope" and hold on.[9]

Carter goes on to share that moms who experience five or more of the following symptoms over a two-week period should seek help.

- Sadness, unhappiness, tearfulness
- Sleeping excessively or being unable to sleep
- Loss of energy
- Loss of interest in things you previously enjoyed
- Irritability

- Difficulty thinking or concentrating
- Sudden change in appetite
- Physical discomfort
- Feelings of worthlessness
- Thoughts of suicide or death

Depression must be treated. If you have more than five of the symptoms listed, seek medical advice right away. And, since we don't always recognize (or don't want to recognize) the symptoms in ourselves, if you notice ongoing symptoms in a mom friend, encourage her to seek help. In the meantime, offer her a rope of friendship and support. Relationships and community make a huge difference when moms are depressed.

FIELD STUDY
More Than Baby Blues

I prepared carefully for Riley's birth, wanting her early experiences to be perfect, but I'm not sure anything can prepare a mom for a severely colicky baby. I was committed to being there for Riley, but after months of steady crying and sleepless nights, I was so sad all the time, finding little joy in my much-anticipated role as a mom.

Although I'm a licensed therapist and have experienced depression in the past, I didn't recognize my symptoms. I guess it was because I was so focused on the mechanics of being a new mom, holding Riley as much as possible, changing diapers, comforting her multiple times through the night, and keeping the breast pump clean. Fortunately, about six months after Riley's birth, one of my friends asked me if I might be experiencing postpartum depression. I consulted a couple others friends who agreed it was a possibility. I made an appointment with my obstetrician who assessed me using the Edinburg PPD test. I scored 21 out of 30. Any score higher than ten indicates the likelihood of postpartum depression. My friends were right.

I was relieved by the diagnosis. It put a name to what I was experiencing and allowed me to cut myself some slack. My feelings of relief were joined by feelings of disappointment because Riley's experience wasn't the perfect one I envisioned. I did ask, "Why me? Why couldn't I have it all together right from the get-go?"

I chose to use medication, saw a counselor, and gave myself permission to leave Riley for a few blocks of time so I had space to rest and heal. A good friend stayed with us for a period of time. Regular naps and exercise also helped. I kept up my counseling practice two days a week and that helped me keep things in perspective. Riley is cared for by her doting grandma on those days. And Riley's doing great! At almost a year old, my word to describe her is atomic! She's so fun and voraciously adventuresome. We're still closely attached physically; she's happily planted on my hip most of the time.

Both as a mom who has been there and as a professional therapist, I want to remind you that we moms aren't infinite but our children's needs sometimes feel like they are. We need each other! In many ways our culture encourages mom disconnect—we drive our own cars, cook in our own kitchens, do laundry in our own laundry rooms, and sit in our private homes raising our kids alone. We must find ways to connect and mother together—co-cook, carpool to the grocery store, take turns doing laundry at one house, and join a mom group. I'm thankful I had friends willing to lovingly help me through a difficult time. You and your child will be happier and healthier if you build strong relationships with other moms. And if they (or you) suspect you're depressed, seek professional help as soon as possible.

—Kelley, mom of one

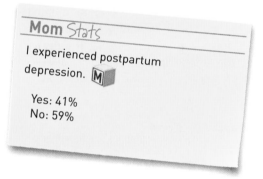

Mom Stats

I experienced postpartum depression.

Yes: 41%
No: 59%

Practicum

* Take a free Edinburg PPD assessment at www.pbhi.com/ global/pdfs/PPD_Brochure.pdf.
* Journal about a time you felt "blue" or possibly depressed. What factors helped change your experience? 🅼
* What family member or friend could you ask to "keep watch" with you?

Quick Review

Knowing myself is important to shaping and maintaining a resilient core.

- Understanding and embracing my innate temperament helps me be a better mom.
- We each enter mothering with a mixed bag of life experiences that need to be embraced and reshaped into the life experiences we bring to our children.
- Assess, assign, and address any negative emotions currently impacting your core.
- Forgiveness prevents long-term damage to your core and is beneficial to shaping resilient moms and kids.
- Depression is a significant health risk to moms and children, so seek treatment immediately if prolonged symptoms occur. Depression is treatable.

1.2 Reinforcing My Core

1.2.1 Strengths and Weaknesses

With a bit of trepidation because they're both teens, I asked my two youngest daughters to share what they consider to be my greatest strengths and weaknesses. They shared that my optimism, perseverance, ability to give good advice and options, along with my good fashion sense were strengths. After I vowed repeatedly that responses would have no impact on the weekly allowance, they shared that my weaknesses included losing my temper too easily, being too controlling, doing too much and getting stressed out, and making them eat Crock-Pot meals.

Just a few years ago, after reflecting on a similar list, my self-talk sounded like this:

> "I'm so controlling, that's why bedtime around here is such a misery."
>
> "Why can't I be more patient? I needed to spend more time doing research before making a decision about schooling."
>
> "I should have spent more time playing with him instead of wallpapering his room in one weekend. I'm just too goal-oriented."

When it comes to self-talk, I now have a different orientation. See if you can figure out what it is.

> "My need to have things under control helped us find a better bedtime routine."
>
> "I had time to visit several schools because I quickly narrowed our overall schooling options."
>
> "How can I use my love of meeting goals to ensure I spend more time with my son?"

Likely you noted my self-talk has a more positive direction. Why? I'm learning to focus on my strengths instead of my weaknesses. Two bits of learning motivated this transformation:

- Working from my strengths is more effective and positive than working from my weaknesses.
- Weaknesses are mostly the flip side of strengths.

Those lessons combine well with two truths that have long shaped my mothering:

- I am wonderfully made.
- I have been specifically designed to match what my child needs in a mom.

If we've been specifically designed to match what our child needs in a mom, it only makes sense to focus on the strengths within that design. Developing our strengths will allow us to be the best moms possible. While being aware of and managing our weaknesses is good, constantly focusing on them is destructive, causing a breakdown in our self-perception and distorting the purposefully and wonderfully designed image we should have of ourselves.

Tom Rath, author of *StrengthsFinder 2.0*, a book based on forty years of Gallup research, says this about working from our strengths: "Our studies indicate that people who do have the opportunity to focus on their strengths every day are six times as likely to be engaged in their jobs and more than three times as likely to report having an excellent quality of life in general." Rath goes on to say, "Gallup's research has shown how a strengths-based approach improves your confidence, direction, hope, and kindness towards others."[10] That's a nice list to reinforce a resilient core, making it well worth the time spent discovering your strengths and using them in everyday life!

Try this. Set a timer for five minutes. Draw a line down the center of a piece of paper. On the left, make a list of your

Mom Stats

My self-talk is usually . . .

Most often critical: 19.8%
Most often supportive: 20.1%
A mixed bag of messages: 60.1%

strengths; on the right, jot down your weaknesses. Which side has the longest list? Likely the one on the right. Most people are more aware of their weaknesses.

If you could choose only one list to cut and paste into your child's brain, which side would you insert? Duh, we'd all choose the list on the left, the one with strengths. (Don't you wish that were possible? It would make this mom thing so much easier!)

Let's make the same choice for ourselves and begin focusing on our strengths. If you haven't done it already, a good place to start is by taking one of the temperament assessments mentioned in 1.1.1. Compare that with the list you just created. What are your greatest strengths? (If you're interested in a more in-depth, research-based assessment, information about StrengthsFinder is in the endnotes.)

VOICES

My greatest strength as a mom is . . .

> Staying calm in stressful or painful situations (at least until the situation has passed).
>
> —Pat, mom of three

> Learning from my mistakes and taking one day at a time because I never know what the next day will bring.
>
> —Meredith, mom of one

Being able to laugh . . . at the kids and their antics, even though sometimes I'd rather scream . . . at myself, especially when I catch myself taking things too seriously.

—Lara, mom of three

My greatest weakness as a mom is . . .

Discipline. I either go overboard or don't remain consistent.

—Eryn, mom of four

Doing everything myself, when I should and could be teaching the kids to pick up after themselves, etc.

—Jolene, mom of two

Learning to let go of my self-conscious ways and inhibitions so I can be silly and fun. There have been many times when we skip a fun activity because I don't want to be seen in a bathing suit.

—Lara, mom of one

Once we know our strengths, we can use them to address the daily needs and larger struggles of mothering. Let's say one mom's greatest strength is being detail-oriented. She can use that strength to arrange playdates for her extremely social kindergartner or to organize a low-cost camping trip when the family needs to get away on a tight budget. At the other end of the spectrum, another mom's strength might be spontaneity. Her spur-of-the-moment decision to take several neighbor kids to the park after school will keep her social kindergartner engaged with friends, and her ability to throw a bag filled with fruit, crackers, and juice in the car and head out to find an adventure will provide fun family outings for next to nothing. Working from their strengths, both moms can achieve great results.

Use your strengths to address the daily needs and bigger challenges of life. Benjamin Franklin said it best:

> Hide not your talents. They for use were made.
> What use is a sundial in the shade?

 Practicum

* My greatest strength as a mom is . . .
* My greatest weakness as a mom is . . .
* How can I change my self-talk about my weakness from negative to positive? Ⓜ

1.2.2 Setting Boundaries

"Yes, yes, yes, yes, yes." While no may be the response we too often give our kids, yes is likely the response moms too often give others. Along with working from our strengths, setting boundaries helps moms reinforce our core. Setting boundaries allows us to make time for the important things of life—mothering our children well, engaging a community of people to help shape our kids, and deepening our relationship with God (we'll cover these in the other three sections of the book). Setting boundaries allows space and time for self-care and personal growth, which we'll explore next.

As moms, we sometimes perceive setting boundaries as selfish, but just the opposite is true. Setting boundaries allows us to be considerate—of ourselves and others. Why is establishing mental, physical, emotional, and spiritual boundaries important to a resilient core? According to Dr. Henry Cloud and Dr. John Townsend, the authors of *Boundaries,* two reasons boundaries are important are (1) to distinguish what is my responsibility and what isn't, and (2) to keep the good in and the bad out.[11]

Setting boundaries encourages good stewardship of resources such as time, energy, money, and space. In terms of children's activities, imagine the difference a good boundary might make in a family. For instance, when a mom—let's call her Tres—decided to spend less time and energy schlepping kids everywhere, she found more time and energy to engage in talking and listening to them. The money saved on activities was put toward a family vacation.

Setting boundaries keeps relationships honest. Tres repeatedly agreed to babysit for her friend, Candace, who hadn't found time to develop a long-term solution to her child-care needs. Did Tres really have time to watch Candace's son so often? Was Candace being honest with herself in putting off a long-term solution? The answer to both questions was no. Their relationship wasn't honest until Tres admitted she was available to babysit only on Tuesday mornings, forcing Candace to take a realistic look at her child-care needs.

Setting boundaries also reduces stress. Tres was stressed all the time when her kids were engaged in too many activities and she was caring for Candace's son as well. She resented the additional demands on her time and was unable to complete her true responsibilities.

Cloud and Townsend suggest that boundaries always involve a support network, someone to give input and encouragement. Support people can also provide accountability to persevere when pushback on a particular boundary undermines confidence. Often boundaries require limiting exposure to certain people who behave poorly toward us. Although the behavior might be harmful, losing the relationship still causes loneliness. A support network helps fill that need for relationship.

Starting with baby steps often makes it easier to create and maintain boundaries, so set a boundary that is fairly easy to stick to. For instance, if your neighbor has totally invaded your time and space, set an initial boundary about knocking and asking permission before entering the backyard. Later on, you could take the bigger step of requesting drop-in visits be limited to late afternoons or weekends.

FIELD STUDY

Just Say No

Not too long ago I was overwhelmed. I was flustered, frustrated, and exhausted because I had overcommitted to too many worthwhile activities, some of which I enjoy quite a bit.

One morning, I remembered I'd agreed to help out with one of my daughter's activities that day. Completely worn out, I flopped on the couch and began my tirade of complaints. "Why did I agree to help out when I already have so much going on?" I listed the many things I had to do. Part of me was hoping someone would recognize my efforts and soothe me. Instead, I'm sure I was quite a spectacle!

My daughters just watched me for a bit. I was hoping for a hug, or maybe they would tell me everything would be okay. But they were hesitant to get too close to me.

Cristina said, "Mom, why don't you just say no to your friends?"

"Yeah, Mom," Victoria chimed in. "After all, you say no to us all the time."

The truth was staring me in the face and I didn't know what to say. I provide healthy boundaries for my girls. I don't let them stay up late and I don't let them get involved in too many activities. I limit their daily TV time, how much candy they consume, and even how many playdates they have each week. Why? Because I understand that too much of a good thing isn't always a good thing.

–Marcie, mom of two

back on the 4 Exercises for Building Resilience sidebar on
boundaries fulfills many of the suggestions.

ime for stress management behaviors
ing to music, and prayer.

ize stress.

tter stewardship of resources, mak-
ore likely in times of crisis.

- ways to communicate needs and
co.

Where d
ndaries in order to reinforce a
resilient core? and Townsend suggest the following areas:

- Family of origin: mom, dad, sisters, brothers, in-laws
- Friends
- Spouse
- Children
- Work
- Self [12]

Practicum

- I have the most trouble saying no to . . .
- How does that lack of boundary affect your ability to mother well?
- What will your child gain if you enforce this boundary? (This might be the motivation you need to persevere if there's pushback.) [M]

1.2.3 Personal Care

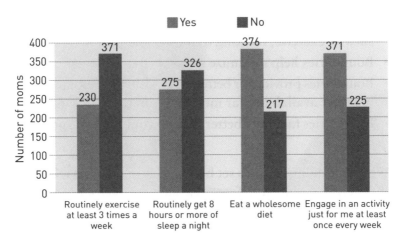

Self-care Survey

Many days, I look out my office window around 11:45 a.m. and see several co-workers enjoying a brisk walk. These moms have found a way to incorporate self-care into their busy lives. (I know, I know. Joining them on the walk would be better for my hips than just watching!)

Watching moms engaged in self-care is refreshing because self-neglect is all too common among moms. We think we're too busy to care for ourselves. Sometimes, we view self-care as self-centered, even wrong. William Shakespeare once wrote, "Self-love, my liege, is not so vile a sin as self-neglecting" (*Henry V*, 2.4.74–75). While the Bard wasn't talking about moms per se, he was right on target with this line.

Self-neglect can inflict some heavy damage to our mom core. Referring to her own recent burnout experience, mom blogger K. Springthorpe posted these thoughts:

> Usually the thing that drops for me is the good habits that keep me healthy. I stay up late, I forget to shower, I don't drink enough water, I can't seem to find the time I need to refresh myself. Instead of doing the things that would actually help to improve my state of mind, I do things that will just help me to feel good right now and get through this moment. I surf the internet instead of washing the dishes. I eat chocolate instead of grabbing a piece of fruit. I let my kids watch more TV instead of taking them out to the park or phoning up a friend with kids. I yell at my children once they are already into mischief instead of stopping their behavior as soon as I see it starting. I do everything wrong.
>
> The more I make the wrong choices, the worse I feel about myself. And the worse I feel about myself, the more I feel defeated by life. And the more I feel defeated by life, the harder it is to think positively and problem solve well, or to deal with my children in a positive and proactive manner.[13]

Springthorpe's post describes what happens when we choose self-neglect instead of self-care. Self-care not only allows moms to deal with their children in a more positive, proactive manner, it models a healthy approach to life.

Just as maintaining a strong physical core requires a multifaceted approach to stretching and exercise, so care for our mom core involves a multifaceted approach to self-care that includes physical, mental, spiritual, and emotional activities. While taking time alone is an important element of self-care, there are also ways to care for self while caring for our children. The chart below offers a few activities to consider, some on your own and others with your kids.

Activities	On My Own	With My Kids
Physical self-care	• Eat healthy, energizing foods and drink enough water • Get enough sleep, even if it means swapping child care or hiring a sitter • Exercise regularly for more energy and to manage stress • Indulge in a hair cut or a home facial, or wear a bright color	• Enjoy a morning fruit break • Snuggle in bed together • Play "Simon Says" using large motor skill movements like jumping and touching toes • Engage in infant or child massage—this relaxes both participants
Mental self-care	• Solve a weekly puzzle—crossword, Sudoku, or other brain teaser • Research a topic • Learn a new skill—knitting, paper-cutting, photography	• Put together puzzles • Take a close look at bugs, eyeballs, trains, or other interesting objects • Learn a new song or play hide-and-seek (you can think while you hide!)
Spiritual self-care	• Maintain a blessings list • Pray • Read a daily Psalm or Proverb • Share an "act of kindness"	• Thank God for the morning • Pray together • Explore a Bible storybook • Share hugs
Emotional self-care	• Have a heart-to-heart talk with a friend • Review your list of strengths • Go on a date night or a girl's night out • Talk with a counselor or mentor	• Draw pictures of a favorite or difficult activity • Share hugs and kisses • Talk about the things you love about each other • Participate in a playgroup

Can you identify one or two ideas from the chart to incorporate into your own life? What might stop you from engaging in those activities, especially the ones in the "On My Own" column? Two common challenges to self-care are lack of motivation and lack of child care. These challenges can often be remedied by engaging other moms in the process. My walking co-workers rely on each other for reminders to walk. If one of them can't walk for several days, the others let her know she is missed. This provides accountability. If child care is a challenge, look for a mom who shares your challenge and take turns watching the kids and taking time for personal care. Or, share the cost of a sitter and do something together!

Mom Stats

Mom's Top 20 Ways to Exercise

1. Walking
2. Playing with my kids
3. Cycling
4. Running/jogging (with or without a stroller)
5. Going to a gym/ YMCA with child care
6. Swimming
7. Pilates/yoga
8. Chasing kids
9. Exercise classes/ personal trainer
10. Exercise DVDs
11. Zumba/dance/ Jazzercise
12. Wii Fit
13. Treadmill/elliptical/ stationary bike
14. Kickboxing
15. Gardening

16. Using my kids as weights
17. Rollerblading
18. Jumping on the bed with my kids
19. Sex
20. Tennis

What about you? Go to www.mom-ology.org and vote for your favorite.

FIELD STUDY

Things That Keep Me Sane

I picked up my phone and dialed my friend, Wendy. I had woken up in a funk the past few days and felt myself spiraling downward emotionally, physically, and in just about every way. I needed to talk to someone, and she's the friend I call when I need a pick-me-up.

"Hi, Wendy. It's Diana."

"Hi. Are you okay? You don't sound like your usual, cheerful self," she said.

"I'm not doing very well." *She always knows*, I thought.

"What's going on?" she asked, not beating around the bush.

We talk for a while and she helps me pinpoint why I'm not feeling well. She knows, and reminds me, that whenever I start feeling run-down or on the edge of losing my sanity, the reason usually boils down to not taking care of me.

A while back I actually made a list of the "Things That Keep Me Sane," reminding me what I need to function best so I can better care for everyone else I love in my life:

- Taking a daily multivitamin
- Spending at least fifteen minutes outside every day, no matter what the weather
- Spending time with God and writing in my journal
- Drinking enough water
- Limiting sugar and processed food
- Eating protein every day
- Spending time with friends at least once a week
- Exercising at least ten minutes every day

- Knowing where I am in my menstrual cycle
- Keeping a positive mindset (I try to think of five positive things when I lay down to sleep)

I'm the kind of person whose rhythm constantly goes up and down, so I've become very self-aware and able to identify what I need for stability. If any of these things on my list are missing or out of balance, I feel it.

—Diana, mom of four

VOICES

Good habits

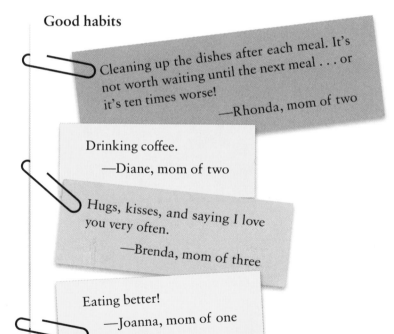

Cleaning up the dishes after each meal. It's not worth waiting until the next meal . . . or it's ten times worse!

—Rhonda, mom of two

Drinking coffee.

—Diane, mom of two

Hugs, kisses, and saying I love you very often.

—Brenda, mom of three

Eating better!

—Joanna, mom of one

Bad habits

Sugar, sugar, sugar! We're trying to keep it down to "one treat a day" . . . but treats are so yummy!

—Elizabeth, mom of two

Watching TV—all my shows are on at the kids' bedtime so I delay that and the kids go to bed late and then get up grumpy. In seven years I have never mastered this.

—Kimberly, mom of two

The guilt I have for everything . . . watching too much TV, staying up too late, not eating well, you name it; for some reason guilt tends to drive me.

—Stephanie, mom of one

Biting my nails!

—Ulli, mom of three

Practicum

* In terms of self-care, one bad habit I'd like to break is . . .
* One good habit I'd like to incorporate is . . .
* What keeps you sane? Share your own list of self-care options at mom-ology.org. [M]

1.2.4 Growing Me

Do you remember the last line in Bonnie's story at the beginning of this book? "By that time, I was involved in supporting other moms of children with serious heart conditions and even started a foundation to raise money for pediatric heart health care."

Out of her mothering situation, Bonnie realized incredible personal growth. Resilience and personal growth are joined at the hip. As moms parent out of their resilience, they experience personal growth. That personal growth develops greater resilience. If you go back and reread Bonnie's story on pages 18–19, you'll note how she engaged with God, with a support system, in learning, and in reaching out to help others. We'll talk more about engaging with God and others in later sections, but for now let's take a look at how engaging the amazing mom brain generates personal growth.

Moms joke about it quite a bit—the idea that motherhood causes brain shrinkage! Truth be told, it also makes us a little nervous when we some-

Mom Stats

Since becoming a mom, I've . . .

Developed more brain cells: 17.2%
Lost brain cells: 58.1%
Stayed about even: 24.7%

times experience symptoms of it. While there is some scientific evidence to support that mom brains shrink by 7 percent during pregnancy, the less reported part of the equation is that if it occurs, this phenomenon lasts less than six months postpartum. After that, moms have just as much brain mass as before, and we often use that mass of brain more effectively than in our pre-mom days.[14]

Whether we're in crisis mode like Bonnie was, or simply searching for creative play, our brains work overtime to fulfill the responsibilities of mothering. We sift through mountains of information on topics as diverse as safe cleaning products and gluten-free snacks. We're forced into creative problem solving when little James ducks under the stall wall to meet our new neighbor in the ladies' room. Plus, we find mental storage capacity for the location of stray socks and immunization records, favorite cereal and tickle spot, times for dentist appointments and. . . . The list goes on and on and on.

Using the amazing mom brain for our kids' sake is part of personal growth, but it's also okay to engage our brain for mom's sake! To develop a skill, live out a passion, or create something new. Often moms don't have a great deal of time for this, but be persistent in taking small steps. Engage your brain in something you're passionate about—environmental issues, teen pregnancy, or women's microfinance projects. Learn to plant a butterfly garden, design a website, or some other interesting new skill. Create a poem or an entrepreneurial business plan. Engaging in personal growth models lifelong learning to our children, opens up options for our own future, and fortifies a resilient core.

Get over the idea that only children should spend their time in study. Be a student so long as you still have something to learn, and this will mean all your life.

—Henry L. Doherty, American businessman

VOICES

I invest in my personal growth by . . .

Making sure that I keep up with new books and music. I take time out from daily life to read or write. This keeps my mind healthy.

—Lisa, mom of three

Hobbies. I have learned to quilt and sew.

—Lisa, mom of three

Building my own home-based business, reading books, and listening to personal growth training.

—Andrea, mom of one

Leading a MOPS group.

—Stephanie, mom of three

Taking some online courses so that when all my kids are in school, I can teach and have the same amount of time with them.

—Brenda, mom of three

Take the First Step

I was cleaning up the mess the high schoolers had made during our youth group meeting when Pastor Mark said, "Liz, I really think you should consider going to seminary. You're so good at working with the youth, and this would really help you in ministry."

His comment took me by surprise. I had been out of school for a while, raising my children, Michael, 8, Sammi, 2, and Joey, my one-year-old. But I was feeling restless and trying to decide what I could do to grow myself and still keep my children a priority. I hadn't thought about going back to school, but my pastor's faith in me lifted my head up just high enough to believe I might be able to do it.

My response surprised me—"Okay, I think I'll look into it." And I did. I took the first step of saying yes and then took the next step of signing up for my first class. A local seminary had just started weekend classes, which worked perfectly for me because my husband traveled all week but was home on the weekends.

As I sat in the classroom the first day, butterflies swarmed in my stomach. I nervously tapped my pencil on the desk and glanced around the room. *I've been out of school for so long, can I really do this?* I thought. I felt out of place. I noticed I was not only the oldest woman in the room but I was surrounded by mostly young men. After a few classes though, my confidence grew, and when I received my first paper back with positive comments, I knew I could do this.

I had to adjust my thinking a little bit from my previous years as a student where I was totally driven by grades and

> performance. During this mothering stage of my life, I decided I was going to learn everything I could and not worry about my grades.
>
> Going back to school developed me as a person, increased my self-confidence, made me more effective in ministry, and helped me be a better mom.
>
> —Liz, mom of three

 ## Practicum

* I invest in learning for my kids' sake by . . .
* I invest (or would like to invest) in learning for my sake by . . .

1.2.5 Developing a Sense of Humor

Humor helps us get along—with emotions, circumstances, people, and our core. I am not a natural comedian, but as a mother I did quickly grasp the value of humor when my friend, Debbie, who was rather particular about hygiene and order, shared a disgusting story about her toddler finger painting the crib with diaper droppings. Debbie could either laugh or cry about the situation, but either way, she had to clean up the mess. Laughter somehow made it easier.

Humor is invaluable in shaping behavior. After several years of attempting to train my children in some of the more complex issues of childhood—such as "If you open a door, shut it," "If you take out the milk, put it back in the fridge," "Towels don't hang themselves up"—one day, instead of plunging into my same old script, I said in total frustration, "It's not rocket science!" In that moment, a more humorous approach that includes launching my right hand off my left arm like a rocket became the new message to clean up your mess.

Silliness can shift a mood that's going south fast. An experience I'll spare you is my disco-opera routine. I'll admit it's scary to outsiders, but when my kids were little my silly self often brought a smile to a sad or pouting face. Nonsense can make the best sense when things get tense. Kids squabbling over whose turn it is to do the dishes? Just let the dog lick 'em. Not really, but just saying it will often press pause on the argument.

Humor acts as a diffuser, a safety valve to let off hard-to-control emotions. It shifts the mood. The Latin root for humor is *umar*, which means "staying fluid and flexible." Humor alleviates stress, freeing our energy for creative problem solving. Here's some advice from Og Mandino:

> Laugh at yourself and at life. Not in the spirit of derision or whining self-pity, but as a remedy, a miracle drug, that will ease your pain, cure your depression, and help you to put in perspective that seemingly terrible defeat and worry with laughter at your predicaments, thus freeing your mind to think clearly toward the solution that is certain to come. Never take yourself too seriously.[15]

Mom Stats

My sense of humor can best be described as . . .

What sense of humor?: 1%
Hit or miss: 56%
Always laughing: 43%

Ideas for Developing a Sense of Humor

- Look for things to laugh about.
- Practice telling jokes.
- Read funny stories.
- Smile more often.
- Seek out funny people.
- Surround yourself with reminders to laugh.
- Laugh when you start to whine.
- Lighten up! Don't take yourself so seriously.

Stumble in front of your co-workers? I'd have free flights for the rest of my life if I got one for every time I trip. And isn't it great that both my hands and my upper arms now wave good-bye together? We need to take ourselves less seriously. There are many worse problems in the world than having wavy arms.

Smile more often. Laugh whenever possible. Shared laughter binds people together, increasing happiness and intimacy. Humor spawns humor. Chuckle, grin, laugh, snort even. It's fun. It's free. It's kid-friendly. Teach your four-year-old to tell knock-knock jokes.

Knock, Knock.
Who's there?
Police.
Police who?
Police stop telling these awful knock, knock jokes!

Just kidding! Keep the jokes and humor, but do police them.

- Avoid hurtful sarcasm.
- Allow time for needed emotions. Sometimes another person needs to cry or express anger.
- Stick with clean humor and watch for innuendo. Set a good example for the kiddos!

Humor is a great stress management tool, a positive, healthy response to the challenges of being a mom. Developing a sense of humor reinforces a resilient core.

FIELD STUDY

Humor Saved My Sanity

I was exhausted. My husband was attending school and working several part-time jobs to support our family. I was home 24/7 with four children ranging from ten to ten months. The baby was not sleeping much and I was praying the others would sleep in a little. A tension headache was crushing my head and I felt cranky and tired and didn't know what could pry me out of this terrible black cloud I was living under. Suddenly I heard two-year-old Sarah's voice.

"Mommeee!" I stumbled to her just as my oldest, Nick, came out of his room.

"Mom, I can watch Sarah so you can sleep," he offered. Did I dare take this chance?

"Just keep her quiet so the baby doesn't wake up."

"You can count on me," he proudly replied as he led Sarah into his room.

I gratefully crept back to my bed. It was so quiet. Then, the whispering began and the scampering between Nick and nine-year-old Libby's rooms. I knew the idea that I could get a little more sleep was too good to be true. I could feel my anxiety and head pain growing. Libby's voice broke through my thoughts.

"Mom, we need you. We can't find the scissors."

Scissors! Why would they need scissors at 7:00 a.m.? I got up and looked into Nick's room to discover little Sarah standing between her older siblings with a big smile on her face and . . . a huge glob of neon green silly putty in her hair. Nick and Libby looked distraught.

"Nick wanted the scissors to cut the silly putty out of Sarah's hair but I figured you could do it more stylishly," Libby seriously explained.

That's when I lost it. I burst out laughing. A great big belly laugh. The tension broke. I couldn't stop laughing as I ran to get the camera. This had to be preserved to share with my husband later today. I was sure he too would need this stress-busting comical moment.

—Barb, mom of four

Practicum

* My sense of humor can best be described as . . .
* I notice the value of humor when . . .
* One thing I could do to develop the family funny bone is . . .
* Humor spawns humor. Share your funny story or picture at mom-ology.org. [M]

Quick Review

Reinforcing our mom core shapes it into something even stronger and more resilient.

* Working from your strengths is more effective and positive than working from your weaknesses.
* Setting boundaries makes room for the important things of life.
* Regularly engaging in holistic self-care is a sound investment in yourself and your kids.
* Mom brains are amazing. Be a lifelong learner.
* Humor lightens the challenges of motherhood.

1.3 Core Value

When God thought of Mother, he must have laughed satisfaction
and framed it quickly—so rich, so deep, so divine, so full of soul,
power, and beauty was the conception.

—Henry Ward Beecher

I'd like to go back to the two truths I shared that have long
shaped my mothering. Here they are again:

- I am wonderfully made.
- I have been specifically designed to match what my child
  needs in a mom.

I praise you because I am fearfully and wonderfully made; your
works are wonderful, I know that full well.

—Psalm 139:14

I am wonderfully made. If you struggle with that statement,
consider your hand for a moment. It has an exquisite design not
found in any other creature. Your hand is in perfect proportion.
Each section of your index finger, from nail to wrist, is larger than
the preceding section by about 1.618%, considered by mathema-
ticians to be the golden ratio. The hand's twenty-seven bones,
combined with joints and nerves and tendons, can flex and move
to make sound and redistribute objects large and small. Your hands
are sensitive enough to estimate whether or not a child has a fever
and to determine the best texture for a blankie. Your hands can
snap to get a child's attention, wipe away tears, and guide a child
safely across the street.

Would God, who so carefully designed the hands that shape children, put any less care into the design and strengthening of a mother's core? Your temperament, your experiences and how you shape them, your emotional reactions, your passions, and your sense of humor—everything about you was put together with purpose.

> For you created my inmost being; you knit me together in my mother's womb.
>
> —Psalm 139:13

> You can be sure that God will take care of everything you need, his generosity exceeding even yours.
>
> —Philippians 4:19 Message

When God knitted you together in your mother's womb, he knew you would one day mother at a particular time, in a particular situation, and, most importantly, with a particular child. When he promises that he will take care of everything you need, he isn't excluding what you need to mother your child well. God's generosity is endless; he's given you all you need to be a great mom to your child.

Out of your specifically designed core, you have the ability to uniquely shape your child, your community, and the world. Take a look at your hand again, this time at the pads of your fingers. Although they look similar to everyone else's, they leave fingerprints that are unique to you. Every mom who has ever lived leaves a unique imprint on her child and her world. Living out of your core, use your influence to leave a positive imprint. In doing so, you will be a better mom who makes a better world.

Me: She's been crying all night. What's bothering her?

Myself: I'm not sure, but I will eventually figure it out.

I: I'm her mom and I've been given all it will take to care for my baby girl.

The Mural

Sandy, a young painter, was asked to contribute to her community by creating a mural on the side of a building in the heart of town. The business owners wanted a piece that represented all that was good in their town. Sandy spent days observing the commuters and pedestrians as they passed by. Finally, with an eye to the finished piece, she began sketching faces, buildings, and interesting objects.

At first, her sketches appeared as unconnected little pieces to those looking on, but she had a vision for how each would fit together. Each day, she sketched a bit more. Sometimes a section failed to live up to her expectations, so the next day she would erase some lines and highlight others, subtly redefining the pictures. Occasionally Sandy removed an entire sketch and started over. On multiple occasions, a passerby criticized her work, saying her design had too much this or not enough that. Discouraged, Sandy would turn back to her original vision and continue painting what she saw.

One day, Sandy stepped back to check her progress and to her surprise, realized she was done. The community mural looked both similar to what she'd originally envisioned and somehow different.

PART TWO

FINESSE

finesse (noun): 1. refinement; 2. subtle or delicate manipulation; 3. artfulness, esp. in effectively handling a difficulty

finesse (verb): artfully rendering the brief sketches that make up our daily routines so that, little by little, they form together into the desired big picture

2.1 Finesse Is Intentional

2.1.1 Picture of Success

Finesse (or the lack of it) shapes the success of our parenting years. As moms, we set high standards for ourselves, and we see ourselves as successful in meeting those standards. At least most of the time. In the 2002 Building Strong Families Study, 34 percent of parents surveyed said they feel successful nearly every day. An additional 54 percent said they feel successful on most days.

When asked how they would define successful parents, those surveyed described someone:

- whose children are respectful, exhibit good behavior, and have good values;
- who gives love to their children;
- who is involved and makes the time to be there for their children;
- who helps their children lead a healthy, productive, successful life.[1]

Finesse requires shaping ourselves as moms so we can shape our children. It involves trying and failing and trying something different, often more than once. Sometimes more times than we'd care to count. Finesse is a somewhat scientific process in which a mom tries out her hypothesis of what she thinks will work, then tweaks it until it actually does work or discards it altogether when it turns out to be a bad match for her family.

VOICES

I feel successful as a mom when . . .

People compliment my children to me. Sometimes I just need a little reminder that they are pretty good, respectful kids because I can get really overwhelmed at times.

—Jill, mom of four

I've connected with my children, cleaned, and taught them something both moral and practical all in the same day . . . oh, and fed them healthy food, too (I don't always feel successful).

—Lydia, mom of two

Not very often . . . this one is really hard for me to answer.

—Sarah, mom of one

I can make it through a day without losing my cool—laughing and loving my children—and have a house that doesn't look like a tornado just blew through it.

—Tracy, mom of three

Practicum

* I feel successful as a mom when . . .

2.1.2 Start with a Big Picture

Shaping ourselves to successfully shape the future begins with envisioning the big picture results we eventually want to see in the little people we're responsible for. It took me a while to understand this.

As a young mom, I was conscientious about knowing and following "the rules"—*very* conscientious.

- Never drive with infant in the front seat.
- Never give in to toddler tantrums.
- Never send food with nuts to preschool.
- Never place man-made materials against baby's skin.
- Never let toddler sleep in parental bed.
- Never allow small children to watch cartoons.

The rules ruled the way I mothered. How well I followed them and how well my little ones responded to me following them determined how successful I was as a mother. Mothering by the rules was supposed to keep my kids safe and ensure that someday in the distant future they would turn out to be healthy, productive big people. Don't get me wrong, rules can be very important. For instance, I fervently advocate car seat safety, and foregoing a lunch box PB&J is a small sacrifice if it protects even one unsuspecting preschooler from anaphylactic shock.

But there were two problems with this approach to shaping children. One, the list of rules kept growing and changing and the experts often had different opinions about the rules. One day I was a good mom because I used a pacifier so my child could put herself to sleep; the next day I was a bad mom racking up huge orthodontic bills.

Two, my kids didn't always respond to rules the way they were supposed to. One day I was a good mom because my well-trained preschooler set the silverware and napkins artfully on the dinner table; the next day I was a bad mom because the same well-trained preschooler set the silverware and napkins artfully next to the dog bowl. And in the dog bowl. And in the dog's mouth.

I felt like a clacker. My dad had one of these in his office when I was a kid. It had five metal balls wired pendulum style in a horizontal row. When I pulled back and let go of the left end, it would hit the remaining four (with a clacking sound which is why I called it a clacker) and swing them to the right. The balls would arc to a high point, then reverse. Watching the metal balls push each other back and forth, back and forth fascinated me. Of course, all this motion never resulted in any forward progress— just clacking.

As a mom, have you ever felt like a clacker? Back and forth, back and forth, in perpetual mothering motion with little forward progress. Watching a toy clacker is fascinating. Mothering like a clacker is frustrating.

Eventually I discovered a better approach. Instead of focusing on following a set of rules, I chose to focus my mothering on the end result, a picture of what I wanted my children to be like when they turned into big people. I took a holistic approach, desiring to influence each child's heart, soul, body, and mind. In my mind,

I developed this big picture filled with the things I deemed most important—things such as faith, family, fun, respect, security, integrity, learning, and independence. Then I became a sketcher, a mother focused on filling that big picture with the intentional daily actions, activities, and attitudes I believed would result in a masterpiece.

I don't want to make this sound easy, because it isn't. There have been countless do-overs and refinements needed. That's part of the forward progress when shaping a masterpiece. As my children grow older, I can see where the picture is smeared, even a bit distorted in places. Despite good intentions, I haven't sketched perfectly. Despite my intentionality, my children sometimes choose to sketch their lives differently. That's part of growing up. However, by changing my approach from mom clacker to mom sketcher, there continues to be intentional forward progress and a freedom from the endless frustration of judging my mothering by "the rules."

Big pictures are best developed in the early days and months of mothering in order to maximize our mom influence. The right time to start creating the big picture of what we want our little people to look like as big people is . . . as early as possible. In fact, begin today if you can carve out some time. If your children are beyond the baby stage, it's still not too late. Schedule time soon to consider this. Include your husband or parenting partner in the process.

Some moms finesse the big picture around character. Others prefer to consider values. Still other moms take their cue from Search Institute's 40 Developmental Assets. To facilitate big picture dreaming, let's look at some of the current thinking on what character, values, or assets might go into that big picture. (For more in-depth information from these experts, check out the books and websites listed in the endnotes for each one.) Then take some time to envision what you'd like your child's big picture to look like. What are the key elements you want to shape for your child as an adult?

Big Picture Results

Expert Take #1

*Developmental Assets
for Early Childhood[2]*

- ☐ Support
- ☐ Empowerment
- ☐ Boundaries and Expectations
- ☐ Constructive Use of Time
- ☐ Commitment to Learning
- ☐ Positive Values
- ☐ Social Competencies
- ☐ Positive Identity

Expert Take #2

*The Six Character Traits
Every Child Needs[3]*

- ☐ Connectedness ☐ Competence
- ☐ Responsibility ☐ Morality
- ☐ Reality ☐ Worship and Spiritual Life

ME

- ☐ _____
- ☐ _____
- ☐ _____
- ☐ _____
- ☐ _____

Expert Take #3

*The Three Driving
Needs of Children[4]*

- ☐ Security
- ☐ Significance
- ☐ Strength

Expert Take #4

Six Pillars of Character[5]

- ☐ Trustworthiness ☐ Fairness
- ☐ Respect ☐ Caring
- ☐ Responsibility ☐ Citizenship

Practicum

* Big picture elements I'd like to see in my child are . . .
* How did you choose the key elements for your big picture? Why are they important to you?

2.1.3 Mom-processing

Mom-processing (noun):
decision making based on information
from multiple sources

VOICES

The biggest decision I made yesterday was . . .

Accurately guessing how to dislodge cheese from my daughter's nostril.

—Sarah, mom of three

Which car seat to buy.

—Nora, mom of four

Whether or not my child should
have surgery.

—Nancy, mom of one

Whether or not to let my daughter stay
another night at her dad's instead of
coming home as planned.

—Jen, mom of one

What to make for dinner!
(Far and away the most common
answer moms shared)

Moms make a multitude of decisions every day—big ones and little ones—that affect the big picture. Mom-processing kicks off with labor and delivery options, shifts swiftly into diapering and feeding, and accelerates rapidly when we start considering discipline and education. Some decisions are quick and easy and we make them intuitively as moms, but others need careful exploration. We have to step back from the masterpiece before making our next sketch. Mom finesse often depends on finely tuned mom-processing skills.

When you have bigger decisions to make, consider this decision-making strategy designed just for moms:

- Identify the purpose or goal of your decision.
- Gather information: use a search engine; talk to friends; check with trusted mentors, spiritual leaders, doctors, family, or other experts.

- Evaluate the information:
  - » Identify principles that might shape your decision.
  - » Brainstorm and list the alternatives you want to consider.
  - » Evaluate your alternatives and determine their costs, requirements, and value.
- Choose the best alternative and create an action plan.
- Take action!
- Evaluate the outcome.
- Own your decision.

What kind of mom-processer are you? In the resource *My Decision-Making Style*, Harvey F. Silver and J. Robert Hanson suggest four distinct styles of decision makers. [6] (If you're not sure which decision-making style you fall into, take their quiz at http://my.ilstu.edu/~kawalst/DecisionMakingStyleInventory.pdf.)

Sequential decision makers need lots of specific information, the details of what's being asked, instructions on the best way of doing things, evidence that particular procedures work best, and steps for doing the task correctly. The sequential decision maker might ask, "What are the steps?" "Where are the directions?" "What's the end result supposed to look like?"

Logical decision makers want the specifics, but more than that they want reasons, defensible positions, and possible results of the different choices. They exercise objective and critical judgment so that choices will not be made based on personal feelings. The logical decision maker might ask, "Have we examined all the possibilities?" "Do we have enough evidence?" "Can we defend our choice(s) based on a critical analysis of all the data?"

Global decision makers want to explore all the possibilities. This process includes what exists and what can be imagined. They are not restrained so much by data as by exploring the possible. The global decision maker might ask, "Isn't there a better way?" "Have we explored all the possibilities?" "What new images need to be created?"

Personable decision makers need lots of specific information, good problem definitions, and the opportunity to explore their own and other people's feelings about the decision(s) being faced. They search for consensus and a feeling of group ownership in regard to process and conclusion. Personable decision makers might ask, "How do I feel about what I'm doing?" "Do I like (dislike) what's happening?" "Is this a good decision for me as well as for others?" "Will this decision be difficult for others to understand and accept?"

FIELD STUDY

Big Decision

Moments before the first time I left my baby A.J. with my mom, I had a meltdown.

I was sitting down to pump breast milk so she could feed him a bottle while I was out, and the reality of my situation hit me like a sharp slap on my face. *In a few weeks I'd be going back to work. I'm going to be leaving him in someone else's care. I'm not the one who's going to be holding him, feeding him, kissing him, singing to him all day long. I can't do this. I really can't do this!* I thought.

I was so tense I couldn't get any milk from my breasts. A puddle of tears pooled in my eyes. I went out to the front yard to find my husband, Tirso. He took one look at me and knew something was wrong.

"*Que paso nena*?" he asked, gently rubbing my back as I sobbed.

"What are we going to do? How are we going to find the right person to take care of A.J. when I go back to work? How am I going to do this? I can't leave him with anyone else."

We'd been over our options many times. Because of decisions we had made, some of which I now regretted, I had to go back to work. We wanted a woman who would come into our home, a woman with day care experience who had mothering experience too. We also wanted her to be Latino because my husband is and we speak Spanish in our home. We wanted someone who would cook and clean so when I got home I could focus on A.J., Tirso, and my stepson. And most importantly we wanted someone who would care for A.J. like I did. It seemed impossible.

"We'll figure something out. You know he's going to be okay," Tirso assured me. "On the days I get off I'll find a way to bring him to you so you can hold him," he promised.

We began our search. We looked at endless applications and finally interviewed seven women. I interviewed each woman in my home for a couple of hours. I wanted to know what she did in her spare time, how she handled stressful situations; I wanted to know her. And then I went to each of these women's homes for a second interview. I wanted to meet her family, see how she really lived.

I guess I would say I'm a "personable" decision maker. I needed tons of information, I needed to share the caregiver's experiences and have her share mine. I wanted to discern her values and have her be intuitive and sensitive to A.J.'s needs. I had to *feel* right about the woman we hired.

After much prayer and searching, we found just the right woman. Before I went back to work she spent time with A.J. and me in our home. I watched her cuddle with him, sing, laugh, and hold him. She met all of our requirements. I felt as comfortable as I possibly could in leaving A.J. with her. I felt we made the best decision we could and know we will continually reevaluate as time goes on.

My first day back to work was incredibly hard. But my husband kept his promise. He brought A.J. to me at lunch and I was able to hug him, smell him, run my fingers through his hair, and kiss him in the middle of the day. I also had peace because I knew he was in good hands when he was at home without either of us.

—Kari, mom of two

Mom Stats

What kind of decision maker are you?

Sequential: 23%
Logical: 41%
Global: 7%
Personable: 29%

Practicum

* I'm a (sequential/logical/global/personable) decision maker.
* One big decision I need to make concerning my child is . . .
* I most often get stuck in the decision-making process because . . .
* To avoid getting stuck with this decision, I will . . .
* Share your mom-processing strategies and dilemmas at mom-ology.org.

Quick Review

Moms intentionally finesse the ins and outs of the daily routine to shape little people into healthy, productive, successful big people.

* Focusing on the big picture is more intentional than focusing on a bunch of mommy rules.
* Mom sketchers invest daily, even hourly, in the big picture.
* Sketching the big picture is a process that includes room for erasing and redrawing.
* Mom finesse is linked to fine-tuned mom-processing skills.

2.2 Finesse—The Work of a Childhood

2.2.1 What's Love Got to Do with It?

What's love got to do with mom finesse? Everything! Our desire and willingness to craft our very lives around shaping a child stems from a deep maternal love. It's like the canvas for our masterpiece, keeping the whole picture together. In her book *The Power of Mother Love*, Dr. Brenda Hunter eloquently writes,

> Ah, the power of mother love. How it stretches and swells across generations, uniting mother and child, fleshing out the expectant mother's identity and femininity, shaping the personality and life of her child, and changing society in ways our culture has chosen to ignore. Mother love is ultimately a love song, a siren's call, luring women to new ways of being . . . to sacrifice and being turned inside out . . . to fulfillment.

A few paragraphs later, Hunter goes on to explain this change mother love brings: "For mother love to be a positive force in a child's life, a woman must move beyond her need for control and her fears of vulnerability. She must grow, as it were, a new heart."[7]

The mother love that developed with the arrival of each of my four children made my heart feel like the Grinch's after he discovered Christmas didn't come from a store.

> And what happened *then* . . . ?
> Well . . . in *Who*-ville they say
> That the Grinch's small heart
> Grew three sizes that day![8]

Like the hearts described by Drs. Hunter and Seuss, my heart stretched beyond my wildest dreams to accommodate the demands and delights of raising each daughter and son. How else could I have ever been willing to sacrifice so much? Because mother love does require sacrifices—the luxury of a full night's sleep; the freedom to run errands with nothing more than keys, license, and debit card; the ability to work or play or just take a shower without interruption; and possibly the most challenging of all, giving up the me-first, my-way mentality that gets in the way of offering unconditional love.

Practicum

* How have I made room in my heart and life to accommodate the demands and delights of being a mom?

2.2.2 Attachment and Bonding

Strong attachment and bonding are critical in the early weeks and months of your mom-child relationship. They provide the base coat in the big picture of a child's life. The Department of HHS identifies early nurturing and attachment as one of the five protective factors known to reduce the risk of child abuse and neglect.

Mom Stats

I bonded with my child . . .

The second I laid eyes on him/her: 75.7%
After a few rough days: 13.8%
Later on, after I'd worked through some things: 10.1%
We've never really bonded: .4%

Expert Take
Benefits of Developing a Strong Mom-Child Bond

- Better academic grades
- Healthier behaviors
- More positive peer interactions
- Increased ability to cope with stress
- Increased brain development
- Balanced body chemistry (resulting in production of essential growth hormones)
- Ability to feel remorse and empathy
- More positive, open, and trusting parent-child relationships
- Easier and more enjoyable parenting[9]

Research shows time and time again that babies who receive affection and nurturing from their parents have the best chance of developing into children, teens, and adults who are happy, healthy, and competent.[10]

Intuitively, most moms realize how much babies need to be held, cuddled, and responded to quickly and appropriately. Two of my children were adopted through the foster care system, and like many foster, adoptive, and stepparents, I've seen firsthand the challenges children face when their primary attachment is disrupted.

My favorite daughter (okay, they're all my favorites) spent her first two years in short, ever-changing living situations, cared for in turn by her birth mom, grandma, aunt, shelter workers, several sets of foster parents, and social workers in a children's home, and then, from age two to almost five, as our foster daughter before her adoption was finalized. Our first visit to the pediatrician revealed she was well below the normal percentiles in height and weight. Way off the chart. Over the next two years, she did not grow. At all. Multiple really-not-fun-for-a-preschooler tests failed to uncover any reason why she did not grow. Finally, her pediatrician told me that if she didn't grow by the next visit, he wanted us to consider growth hormone therapy, even though the tests indicated her hormone levels were normal. Honestly, I was ready to try anything. At that next visit three months later, my daughter had grown more than two inches. Puzzled, the pediatrician asked if anything had changed in her diet or routine.

"The only change," I told him, "is that we were given permission to adopt her right after our last visit."

"Does she know?" he asked.

"Yes, we told her right away and retell her almost every day."

"That's it then," he told me. "She's finally found a safe place to grow."

Since that moment, I've never underestimated the value of mom-child attachment.

In their book *Raising Great Kids*, Henry Cloud and John Townsend discuss how attachment happens.

> Specific tasks create the ability to connect. The child has his job, and the mother (or the primary caregiver) has hers. These two jobs interact to help the child become capable of making attachments to people.
>
> The child must experience the reality that relationship is good and that it brings the necessary elements of life. When your child learns this emotionally, he structures his existence to seek rela-

tionship to sustain him. He becomes relationally-oriented rather than self-oriented.

The mother's task is to invite her child from isolation into relationship. This invitation, or wooing of sorts, takes many experiences in order to bear fruit. The mother behaves and responds to the child in a fashion tailored to his particular situation and need. For example, she pays close attention to her child's differing cries, so as to meet his appropriate need for comfort, warmth, changing, or safety. He learns during these times that reaching outside himself for help brings things he needs.[11]

Attachment happens when moms are:

- Loving—Offer an unconditional love that gives time, energy, and yourself to meet a child's emotional and physical needs.
- Touchable—Get physical! Snuggle, hug, kiss, massage, stroke, grasp fingers, tickle toes, massage temples, rub cheeks, wear baby in sling.
- Available—During the early months, give as much undivided attention to your baby as possible. As your child grows older, continue to connect frequently in response to your child's current needs. Attachment is a matter of quality and quantity.
- Predictable—Be known as the loving presence that routinely dries wet bottoms and dispenses warm drinks in the night, the strong arms that regularly envelope and sway fussy dispositions, the laughing personage who readily sings silly songs and blows raspberries to relieve boredom.
- Responsive—Study your child. Get to know what his cries and expressions mean and how you can best respond. Be patient

with yourself. This learning can be hit-or-miss, especially at first. I have yet to meet a mom who got it right every time.

- Intuitive—Listen to what your heart says and respond accordingly, whether or not it's what everyone else is doing.

Shaping our schedules to allow as much time as possible for attachment is important. Does this mean a mom must be with her child every waking moment? What does a mom do if she is working, managing physical or emotional challenges, has older children, or for some other reason needs to be away from her child for periods of time?

- Be present as much as possible.
- Let go of guilt. Think both/and instead of either/or. Attending to the financial and physical needs of the family and taking time for self-care can be combined with nurturing strong attachment.
- Select the alternative care arrangement that best mirrors your own mothering to provide baby with the most predictable environment.
- Leave a little of yourself behind, something that has your scent, such as a sleep shirt, pillowcase, or breast milk.

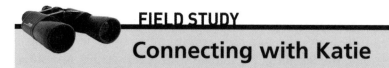

FIELD STUDY

Connecting with Katie

I wonder when we will get to meet her, I thought as I signed the stack of adoption papers for our Chinese daughter, Katie.

I sat in a stark conference room at a long, skinny dark wood table with my husband Ken, our interpreter, a government worker, and another couple who were also adopting a daughter.

When I heard a little movement over my shoulder, I looked around and there stood Katie. Ken didn't even have the camera ready. This was not at all how I envisioned our first meeting.

My eyes met hers and she let go of the man's hand and started yelling, "Mama!" She ran right to me with her hands up in the air. She was wearing a white top and a traditional pink Chinese coat with teeny tiny cloth-covered buttons. In her arms she carried the little doll we had mailed.

I scooped her up and held her. I felt her thick black hair under my chin and smelled her fresh soapy scent. *My little girl*, I thought with tears streaming down my face.

I knew Katie's attachment to us would likely take some figuring out. For example, I created a calm, peaceful room with a fuzzy yellow comforter and soft yellow paint for her. Our first night home, I kissed her night-night and slipped out of the room, gently closing the door behind me. A few moments later I heard whimpering. I opened the door and she was sitting in a sea of yellow, crying—terrified to be alone. That night my husband and I decided one of us would stay with her until she fell asleep.

Building trust with Katie has to be very intentional. We work on physical connection to build trust, including feeding by hand to reassure her of sufficient food and kneeling down to talk with her so we have eye contact. We pretend play with baby dolls. While we're playing I say things like, "This is what mommies do, mommies feed babies and mommies kiss their babies." Both Ken and I stayed close at all times for the first two months.

I know, in time, the attachment will come.

—Bev, mom of three

VOICES

To deepen the attachment I have with my child, I . . .

Just stay still and listen. Both my kids have this incredible gift of gab. While very little of it makes any sense, it means something to them.

—Cosette, mom of two

Get on the floor and play with them.

—Tara, mom of three

Nursed as long as possible and let them sleep with me on occasion.

—Joanna, mom of three

Try my best to spend time with them as individuals. Two of my kids are more like me, so it's not difficult with them. The third is very different from me, and I struggle most with her in having a close relationship.

—Sara, mom of three

Snuggle and kiss them as much as possible.

—Autumn, mom of two

Practicum

* The first time I really bonded with my child was when . . .
* One of the challenges I've faced in attachment is . . .
* My own childhood attachments are impacting the way I mother by . . . [M]

2.2.3 Time Well Spent

Spend the afternoon; you can't take it with you.

—Annie Dillard

Mom-child attachment continues to be important even after the initial bonds are forged, calling us to regularly and routinely invest time in shaping our children through intimate, loving relationship. When children are small, their adult selves seem light years away. It appears as if there's an unlimited amount of time to determine how we'd like those adult selves to look. While there is *plenty* of time to sketch into the lives of our kids, *time has limits*.

I heard a story once about a young mom complaining to an older mom about never having fun with her preschool-age son.

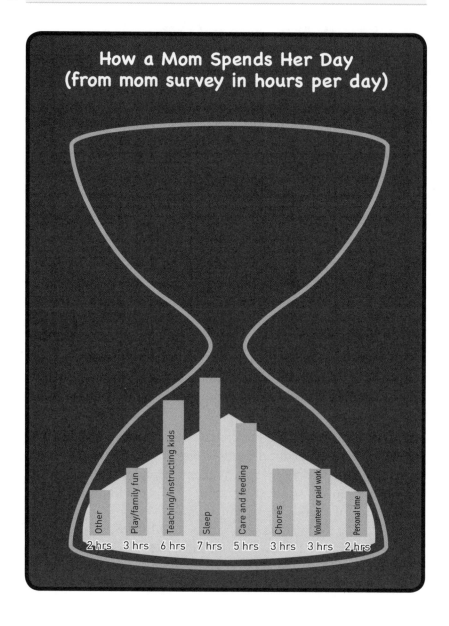

When the older mom asked what the family did on weekends, the young mom shared, "Errands and housework." The older mom gently informed her friend that every childhood holds only 936 weekends, asking her to estimate how many weekends had been spent so far on errands and housework. Since the little guy was almost four, it turned out to be just over two hundred. Shocked by how many precious weekends were already gone, the young mom reevaluated, choosing to spend a higher percentage of weekend time on activities that would build the childhood memories she wanted to shape her son's life.

Spending time with our kids doesn't always revolve around organized fun. Even a weekend spent on home improvements can be family oriented if children are included in the work. When cleaning a room, ask your child to dust the baseboards or push the Swiffer. While grocery shopping, engage preschoolers in selecting fruits and vegetables. There are many ways to engage small children in routine tasks. This not only increases the time you have together, it prepares them for managing a household of their own someday.

VOICES

My "wish list" for fun family weekends includes . . .

A leisurely Saturday morning pancake breakfast, a picnic at the park, watching my children's baseball game, and an evening out to get ice cream.

—Pamela, mom of three

Theme parks! We love going to theme parks.

—Melissa, mom of two

A spur-of-the-moment trip where we stay at a hotel and see fun sights along the way.

—Melia, mom of two

Team-spirit chore completion, followed by some fun activity either out or at home.

—Sharon, mom of three

Hiking, spending time together in the backyard, going on a "daycation."

—Shari, mom of three

Practicum

* How many weekends has my child experienced?
* What percentage of our weekends are spent participating in a fun family activity?
* My wish list for future fun family weekends includes . . .
* Share your wish list at mom-ology.org. Ⓜ

2.2.4 Getting a Grip on the Dailies

A reality for mothers is that if we're not careful, the dailies can consume every waking moment (and most of the sleeping moments, too). If the daily routines become daily challenges, it will be hard to find time to work on the biggies. The scientific process you used to complete that fifth grade science project can make managing the dailies take less of the day.

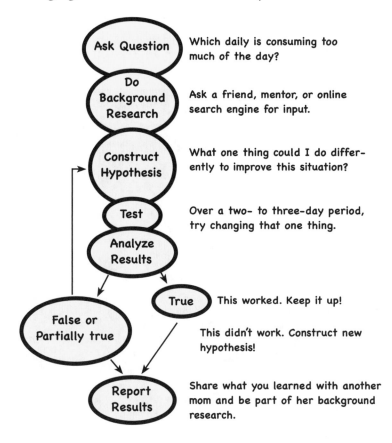

Ask Question — Which daily is consuming too much of the day?

Do Background Research — Ask a friend, mentor, or online search engine for input.

Construct Hypothesis — What one thing could I do differently to improve this situation?

Test — Over a two- to three-day period, try changing that one thing.

Analyze Results

True — This worked. Keep it up!

False or Partially true — This didn't work. Construct new hypothesis!

Report Results — Share what you learned with another mom and be part of her background research.

In talking about this method, sciencebuddies.org says, "Even though we show the scientific method as a series of steps, keep in mind that new information or thinking might cause a scientist to back up and repeat steps at any point during the process. A process like the scientific method that involves such backing up and repeating is called an iterative process."

Finessing the dailies is very much an iterative process, much like sketching. Franklin D. Roosevelt offers this bit of advice you may find useful in keeping the dailies from overtaking the biggies: "It is common sense to take a method and try it. If it fails, admit it frankly and try another. But above all, try something."

A Mom's List of Daily Duties

- Getting out of bed
- Choosing clothes for the day
- Collecting gear for the day
- Fixing breakfast, lunch, dinner (at least snacks are easy!)
- Brushing teeth (and hair)
- Putting on socks and shoes
- Putting away toys
- Buckling car seats
- Looking both ways when crossing street
- Handling back talk
- Shutting down whining
- Preventing biting
- Keeping an eye on kids
- Facilitating playdates
- Cleaning just about anything
- Feeding pets
- Preparing for bed

Practicum

* Currently, my biggest daily challenge as a mom is . . .
* Find a buddy and take your challenge through the scientific process. What's your hypothesis (potential solution)? What did you learn that will help you with this challenge?
* Discuss your challenges and solutions at mom-ology.org. Ⓜ

2.2.5 The Family Calendar

Worthwhile activities get crammed into the pages of our family calendars like a troop of clowns piling into a little circus car. Unlike the clown car, a stuffed calendar isn't very funny. Stuffed calendars cause stress and make it difficult for families to connect. Stuffed calendars are a primary cause of what child psychologist David Elkind describes as "the hurried child," a child with too many activities and not enough childhood. In his book *Ties That Stress*, Elkind describes the postmodern home this way: "Home is no longer a haven, a place for nurturance and protection. Rather it is more like a railway station, with parents and children pulling in and out as they go about their busy lives."[12]

Clown cars and railway stations imply a constant go-go-go that crowds out time for resting, thinking, connecting, and experiencing childhood, all of which are imperative to sketching the big picture. As moms intent on shaping the future, we want our calendars to be more like corrals, defensive enclosures that create space for who and what we deem important while providing a barrier to keep out unnecessary or even harmful things. Without those unnecessary or harmful things in the family calendar, you leave empty spaces in the big picture of your children's lives. As you play the role of gatekeeper for the family calendar, keep the following ideas in mind:

- Keep it visible. One mom painted a huge whiteboard calendar on her kitchen wall. Moms without the space (or inclination) for that can post a more traditional calendar on the refrigerator or on a wall in a high traffic area. Select a calendar that has enough space to accommodate everything.
- Keep it up. Allow time in each day's schedule to schedule. Write down the actual event and any time needed to prepare

for the event. For instance, when you're scheduling your book club, don't forget to schedule time to read the book.

- Post a week or a month at a time. Often we don't realize how busy we are until we look at our days in the larger scope of a week or a month and in the context of other family commitments.
- Schedule "nothing" time. Down time. Keep your eye on this one or it will slip away!
- Schedule family time. Whether it's a night at home together or a Saturday morning activity, plan a consistent time to do things as a family.
- Limit individual activities. With multiple children, especially young ones, the limit may need to be one. In the case of activities, even 1+1 sometimes equals 2 many!

FIELD STUDY

Less Means More

So many families sign up their children for all sorts of organized activities at an early age to help them find friendship, have fun, and excel at something. My husband and I have worked hard at doing the opposite. We want our children to learn to just play without the pressure of adults telling them how to do this. So, we decided to delay organized activities until first grade rather than at three or four years old. I'm glad we've done this because our children have learned to have fun, make friends, and play without any pressure to perform.

—Julie, mom of three

VOICES

My favorite tip to corralling the family schedule is . . .

Try to keep it as loose as possible. Little kids need flexibility and plenty of boredom (it helps improve their creativity!).

—Darcy, mom of three

I keep the calendar in plain view. When I start seeing more black than white in the squares we have to start saying no more!

—Stephanie, mom of three

Keep an updated, online calendar. With kids, events change all the time. A virtual calendar can be altered quickly without mess and printed as needed.

—Rebecca, mom of two

Not to schedule TOO much. Kids get burned out if they don't have any down time. (Adults do too!)

—Jennifer, mom of two

Practicum

Record yesterday's schedule on the calendar below.

* How much time was allocated for "nothing" and how much for family?
* How well does the way you spent time yesterday match what you want to sketch for your kids?
* Share your favorite ways of corralling time at mom-ology.org. Ⓜ

1 a.m.	
2 a.m.	
3 a.m.	
4 a.m.	
5 a.m.	
6 a.m.	
7 a.m.	
8 a.m.	
9 a.m.	
10 a.m.	
11 a.m.	
NOON	
1 p.m.	
2 p.m.	
3 p.m.	
4 p.m.	
5 p.m.	
6 p.m.	
7 p.m.	
8 p.m.	
9 p.m.	
10 p.m.	
11 p.m.	
MID	

2.2.6 Traditions

Swimsuits, flip-flops, and sunscreen come in Easter baskets. Mickey Mouse pancakes are for breakfast when friends sleep over. Family Night always includes a round of "Peak and Pit" (see below for an explanation of this fun tradition). While these factoids may seem odd to some, for my children they are part of growing up Radic.

Traditions encourage families to spend time together and provide time for strengthening family attachments. For children, they become things to count on in an ever-changing world. For moms, traditions are important tools for sketching indelibly into our children's lives.

Traditions—

- Teach and affirm family values and faith
- Provide time to celebrate both individual family members and the family unit
- Encourage family communication
- Honor the passage of time
- Provide ties to cultural identity
- Create links to distant family members and past generations
- Form shared memories
- Provide continuity and comfort
- Promote family fun

*Peak and Pit. This game is one of my favorite family traditions. Each family member shares the best thing (peak) and the worst thing (pit) about their day or week. Peak and Pit might also provide a fun way to sort out your extended family traditions. With your hubby or perhaps a group of mom friends, share the peaks and pits of family traditions from your growing-up years. Select one or two of the "peaks" to bring forward into your own family.

Traditions can be grouped into three main categories:

Daily traditions—waking up to a special song, revolving chore
 charts, 5 p.m. phone call with traveling parent, bedtime song
 and prayer . . .
Family traditions—first day of school photos, planting fall
 bulbs, hot chocolate on rainy mornings, Friday night camping in the living room . . .
Holiday traditions—going for a hike after church on Mother's
 Day, fall decorating with pumpkins and leaves, making mon-
 key bread for New Year's breakfast, being "surprised" with
 new pajamas on Christmas Eve . . .

With traditions we're often tempted to believe more is better.
Take it from a mom who learned the hard way, more means stress.
For most moms, it's best to finesse traditions by selecting just a
handful from each category; those few traditions you believe will
be meaningful, fun, and likely to stick over the years. Come from
an extended family with enough traditions to fill a phone book?
Pare the list down to those most important to your immediate
family. If a tradition doesn't make your A list but it's important
to your mother or mother-in-law, schedule time for her to share
it with the kids.

VOICES

Peak and Pit Traditions from Moms

Peak

Picking a different country each New Year's Day and creating a meal from that culture.

—Karrie, mom of two

Making tamales at Christmastime.

—Irene, mom of one

Planting sunflower seeds every summer and taking pictures with the children as the flowers grow.

—Mamie, mom of two

Our Christmastime "Pajama Raid" night that my husband and I put the kids to bed as usual, then about five to six minutes later we run in yelling "Pajama Raid!" We bundle everyone into the car and drive around looking at Christmas lights.

—Sharon, mom of three

Pit

Easter morning candy chow down—
toooooo much sugar makes everyone
wonky by noon!

—Sherri, mom of three

When we drive out to the lake for our
yearly trip, the car ride is ALWAYS horrible because our kids don't do long car
rides well at all!

—Nikia, mom of two

The arrival of the tooth fairy. She is notorious
for forgetting our house, getting lost, or being
seriously late!

—Gini, mom of five

 ## Practicum

* My peak tradition growing up was . . .
* Three traditions I think will be meaningful, fun, and will
  stick for my family are:

  Daily—   Family—   Holiday—
* Discuss traditions at mom-ology.org.

Quick Review

Moms shape their children through intentionally creating and illustrating in a strong, loving relationship.

- Mother love is a powerful, sacrificial, life-shaping force.
- Maximizing time for attachment and bonding, especially in the early stages of a child's life, is foundational for healthy, well-adjusted kids.
- Getting a handle on the dailies leaves time for the biggies.
- Taking control of the family calendar deters the family calendar from taking control of family life.
- Repeated family traditions are tools that indelibly sketch shared family memories.

2.3 The Finesse of Actions and Words

2.3.1 Doing What I Say and Saying What I Do

The mother's heart is the child's schoolroom.

—Henry Ward Beecher

Our little people mimic both our good stuff and our bad stuff. They rarely miss a trick when it comes to the bad stuff. If you don't believe me, try sneaking in a negative comment about your neighbor's kids. It won't be long before you overhear a little voice in the front yard repeat, "My mommy says Baxter kids (surname has been changed to protect me from further embarrassment) are mean so I can't play with you anymore." Yep, the Baxter kids' mom was standing there, too.

Our kids learn from our words, but they learn even more from our actions. If we say we're going to sketch patience but then really draw impatience, we know what our kids will really see. The deepest learning of all comes when there's a match between actions and words. It's a match when we say breakfast is the most important meal of the day and then sit down with them over a banana and a bowl of cereal. It's not a match when we tell a child to use gentle words and then scream at his dad for forgetting to bring home eggs and diaper wipes.

VOICES

The most embarrassing "repeat after mommy" my child ever shared was . . .

One day while pushing my son in the "race car" cart down the canned vegetable aisle in our grocery store, an elderly woman stopped in front of us to grab a can of corn off the shelves. My son started to "honk" the race car horn and yelled, "Move it, Grandma!"

—Ashli, mom of two

My daughter's preschool teacher asked her if she was thirsty and if she'd like a drink. My daughter responded, "I'll have a double shot on ice." (Thankfully her teacher knew she was talking about Starbucks and was only ordering my favorite coffee drink.)

—Brandi, mom of two

> My husband came home from work one day and asked my three-year-old how the day went. In his sweet three-year-old voice he said, "Well, Daddy, the #@&% ants are back!" And they were. These little ants manage to sneak in our house every spring.
>
> —Julie, mom of five

 Practicum

* What word or action that you use regularly might cause an embarrassing moment if repeated? How can you break the habit of using it before it's too late?
* Share your embarrassing moment at mom-ology.org. [M]

2.3.2 Information Please!

It's a big job to be a child's first and most influential teacher. Oddly, we step into what is arguably the biggest job of our entire lives with negligible training. How's a mom supposed to know what to say and do and how to respond? How do we find finesse to do this job well? Who is teaching the teacher?

Parenting 411 for moms flows primarily from six sources (not necessarily in order of importance!):

- Self
- Experts
- Peers
- Mentors
- The Bible
- Our kids

Self. Each mom has a built-in body of knowledge made up of life experiences, education, and her own intuition about what her child needs. Noted pediatrician Dr. William Sears reassures moms when he states, "God would not have given you this child without also giving you the means to care for this child."[13] Although difficult to quantify scientifically, mom intuition plays an important role in how we care for and teach our children. Mom blogger Elizabeth puts it beautifully:

> I believe we all are equipped with instincts specific to each of our children. I know our lives these days are fast paced and hectic, but what better reason to slow down and smell the roses. We need to take the time to tune in to our children and let our instincts develop. It took me a long time to start consistently listening to my mother's intuition. I wish I would have sooner. I think I could have saved my son from dealing with a lot of the issues he has had to deal with in life. None of them are terrible or life threatening but his life would have been a whole lot easier had I tuned in to what he needed earlier on. But, over time I have learned to trust that nudging feeling and not ignore it. It is so important, as moms,

that we use all tools available to us to best meet the needs of our children.[14]

Experts. There's no shortage of parenting experts. Besides those experts we interact with on an up close and personal basis—such as our own mom, pediatricians, and our child's preschool teacher— kid experts are regular features on radio and television talk shows, author a prolific number of books and magazine articles, and host web pages and blogs. In this Wikipedia world where just about anyone can say she's an expert, how can a mom differentiate who's in the know from who just thinks she knows?

- Do a background check. What are her credentials (mom experience or education)? Is she respected in her field and family? How has her advice been tested? What are her basic values? Are they a match with your own?
- Research other options. What are other opinions on the subject? For example, there are several opinions on vaccinations. Weigh all the options before making a decision.
- Use discernment. This is where mom intuition comes in again. If something seems off to you, trust your instincts. Consider whether or not the advice matches your values. Does it line up with God's Word?
- Test it out. If the expert measures up and the advice makes sense for your situation, try it. If it works well, include it in your "files." If it doesn't, click delete.

Peers. Moms soon discover some of the most tried and true, practical advice around comes from moms at the park, moms in your MOPS group, moms in your neighborhood, moms you friend on Facebook, and moms you bump into in the diaper aisle when your two-year-old is having a meltdown over not getting to chew on your cell phone. Networking regularly with mom friends provides a steady stream of ideas, mom-tested tips, and women "in the know" to compare notes with when you're looking for information.

Mentors. In the not-so-distant past, young moms lived close enough to their own moms, aunts, and older sisters that a seasoned mom was always just around the corner. While you can Skype your mom or big sister just about anywhere in the world, sometimes it helps to have someone experienced you can talk with face-to-face. Whether it's your mom or someone else, consider finding a mentor, a woman further along in the mom adventure who can offer her expertise when you need it. The nice thing about a mentor's expertise is she'll know you, your child, and your values well enough to offer a personalized approach to the information you're seeking.

The Bible. As I've searched for information to help me be a better mom, I've discovered the Bible offers better mom information than a search engine. Search God's Word on a daily basis for life-giving words to mother by. Below is a little glimpse of what you can find.

- For kids (or moms) struggling to complete a job with excellence—

  > Don't just do the minimum that will get you by. Do your best. Work from the heart for your real Master, for God.
  >
  > —Colossians 3:23 Message

- For days when worry is a constant companion—

  Do not worry about your life, what you will eat or drink; or about your body, what you will wear. . . .Look at the birds of the air; they do not sow or reap or store away in barns, and yet your heavenly Father feeds them. Are you not much more valuable than they?

  —Matthew 6:25–26

- For those times when you can't get to everything—

  There is a time for everything, and a season for every activity under heaven.

  —Ecclesiastes 3:1

- For responding to whiny kids—

  Do everything without complaining or arguing.

  —James 2:14

Our kids. Invest time and thought into "learning" your child. Her gifts, challenges, thought patterns, and favorites have been uniquely and carefully designed. They offer clues on how to shape her future. And remember, kids are also great teachers. Whether it's how to identify dinosaurs or how to love the homeless person on the street corner, our kids often have fresh insights and ideas to enrich and enlarge our lives.

Mom Stats

When I need parenting advice, I most often go to . . .

Variety of experts: 37%
My mom/mom-in-law/
   grandmother: 20%
Friends/other moms: 19%
God/Bible: 8%
Self/husband: 6%
Children's Response: 3%
Sister/sister-in-law/cousin: 2%
Pastor/pastor's wife: 1%
Other: 4%

Practicum

* One source of advice I'd like to develop is . . .
* The best thing I've learned from my child is . . .
* Share your favorite advice at mom-ology.org. Ⓜ

2.3.3 Managing External Influences

As our children grow older, more and more influences vie for their attention. In a recent study, researchers found that mothers seem to hold values that differ in significant ways from those of the larger culture.

- 95 percent agree that they wish American culture made it easier to instill positive values in children.
- 88 percent expressed concern about the influence of media on children.
- 87 percent expressed concern about the influence of advertisements on children.
- 86 percent agreed that childhood should be a time

Mom Stats

Top 20 Things Moms Have Learned from Their Kids

1. Unconditional love
2. Patience
3. The beauty in the little things
4. I'm not perfect, but I am still a good mom
5. Trust/depend on God
6. God's love for me
7. To watch what I do and say, because they'll do and say it too
8. Flexibility
9. Have fun
10. Relax
11. Perspective
12. Slow down
13. Don't sweat the small stuff
14. How to see things from someone else's point of view
15. I don't have all the answers
16. Selflessness
17. How to function when sleep deprived
18. The value of a nap
19. Thankfulness
20. My mom was right after all

when children are protected from large parts of the adult world.[15]

When we consider all the negative influences children might be exposed to, the idea of surrounding our innocent babes with an impermeable bubble can look very attractive. Common sense (and our own experiences as teenagers) tells us that children will not willingly live the bubble life forever. They will want and need to engage with the world around them. And the world holds many positive influences we want our children to embrace and experience. Protect and engage. How do we finesse both?

IMMERSE IN EXCELLENCE

- Engage kids in the best your culture has to offer. Immerse them in selected music, art, literature, science, and physical activities to develop an awareness of and attraction toward excellence.
- Surround kids with great people of all ages, people who live out your family values and invest their lives in making the world a better place.
- Communicate your values in real time. In the grocery store, allow someone to go ahead in line, purchase food for a soup kitchen, share why you bring reusable bags, take only one free cookie from the sample plate, and stick to your budget.
- Invest in what's right. Race for the Cure. Host an international student. Clean the church nursery. Support an at-risk child.
- Introduce kids to a variety of cultures, allowing them to experience the many foods, music, traditions, and art of the world.

Instill discernment

- Identify negative influences and discuss why they are harmful.

- Practice making safe responses, such as how to say no, move away, tune out, or seek assistance.

- Teach evaluative skills. Is this real or pretend? True or false? Good or bad? Safe or scary? For young children, the choices need to be simple.

- Listen and communicate. Take time to understand how your child is thinking and share your own thinking.

- Be aware. As a mom, develop ways to keep up with the culture through online newsletters, networking with friends, and attending parenting conferences.

With 88 percent of moms concerned about the influences of media, I asked Kari Glemaker, mother of three and National Director for iCare, a division of the National Coalition for the Protection of Children and Families, to share insights on how she and her husband, Dave, handle media and other outside influences with their three kids. While Kari shares primarily about handling the influences of technology, the principles she offers can help moms get a handle on many of the outside influences impacting families today.

As parents, we are the number-one influencers in our children's lives. When your children are little, figure out family standards and *communicate them regularly* so these standards become their norms. One short talk on a subject is not enough. As moms, we have to *take a good look at our own lives*, how much time we spend on the phone, how we interact online, what types of programs we watch on television. Our children are watching and learning from our example.

Use parental controls wherever possible, on phones, computers, portable game devices, television. Set these at an appropriate level for your child. Check the history regularly. Parental controls like Covenant Eyes not only block requested information, they notify parents if someone tries to breach the filter. Let your kids know this is a way you help them develop their own moral compass. *Set time limits* for engagement with screens and enforce them. This teaches time management skills and leaves time for other activities like outdoor play and reading.

Keep all screens in public areas. Remember, game devices and cell phones and computer systems may allow internet access. Engage in appropriate media with your kids. *Make it a family activity.* There are great opportunities for learning, exploration, connecting, and having fun together. Be aware. Know what and who your kids are interacting with. Ask questions until you're satisfied with the answers. And provide kids with tools for how to respond if something comes up that doesn't meet the family standards. *Role play* works great for this.

For more suggestions, check out the iCare website at www.icare coalition.org.

VOICES

To engage my family in the best our culture has to offer, I . . .

Try new foods, discuss ethnicities, and encourage them to play with kids who are far different from them.

—Diana, mom of three

"News Time." We like to find important news messages on the internet and share them in a less violent manner. We then talk about their feelings on the subject and ask them to relate.

—Cami, mom of two

Play Spanish TV and radio to expose them to my culture, and telling the stories that grandparents told us about our *tradiciones*.

—Josie, mom of five

One way I protect my kids from negative influences is . . .

Only having a computer in rooms that can be supervised at all times.

—Melissa, mom of two

Communicating—a lot! We don't isolate them, but we try to help them create boundaries and borders in their lives.

—Coral, mom of three

Get to know their friends and volunteer in their classroom, keep in close contact with teachers. I talk to them about what they see and hear. If we talk about the little things now, I hope we will be able to talk about bigger things as they get older. PRAY.

—Lori, mom of two

Practicum

* What are the positive influences I want to include in my child's life?
* How are my kids vulnerable to negative influences right now?

2.3.4 Discipline

I Googled discipline and got 85,700,000 results. By narrowing the search to child discipline techniques, the list was reduced to a mere 16,600,000 sources. This supports my hunch that one-size-fits-all discipline is about as probable as one-size-fits-all jeans. (And we've all tried on enough pairs of jeans to know how likely that is!) Step-by-Step How-to Manuals, 1-2-3 Magic Instructions, 5 Pointers— wouldn't it be nice if discipline was that easy to finesse?

A look at the word *discipline* helps us understand the importance of wading waist deep through discipline techniques to find those we can utilize with great mom finesse.

discipline (noun): the practice or methods of teaching and enforcing acceptable patterns of behavior

discipline (verb): to make yourself act or work in a controlled, systematic way

As moms, teaching and enforcing acceptable patterns of behavior (the noun) shapes children who can act or work in a controlled, systematic way (the verb)—children who, according to another definition of the noun form, will have "the ability to behave in a controlled and calm way even in a difficult or stressful situation."

In an online survey, moms responded to the following statements about discipline as follows:

- My approach to discipline consistently produces positive, productive outcomes.
    Agree: 77%
    Disagree: 23%
- I play the most important role in my child's discipline.
    Agree: 89%
    Disagree: 11%
- Disciplining myself to engage in consistent, productive discipline is one of my greatest challenges as a mom.
    Agree: 82%
    Disagree: 18%

What do you think?

As a mom, I agree with all three statements, but to be honest, sometimes I don't want to discipline. Discipline is hard to finesse. It takes time, energy, resourcefulness, perseverance, and . . . well . . . discipline. Two timeless truths from the book of Proverbs encourage moms to keep at it.

> Good friend, follow your father's good advice;
> don't wander off from your mother's teachings.
> Wrap yourself in them from head to foot;
> wear them like a scarf around your neck.
> Wherever you walk, they'll guide you;
> whenever you rest, they'll guard you;
> when you wake up, they'll tell you what's next.
> For sound advice is a beacon,
> good teaching is a light,
> moral discipline is a life path.
>
> Proverbs 6:20–23 Message

When discipline yields the dreaded "You're so mean, I hate you!" from a child, a second truth provides perspective.

> A refusal to correct is a refusal to love;
> love your children by disciplining them.
>
> Proverbs 13:24 Message

Loving a child through discipline is a science that requires careful observation of our kids—their patterns of behavior, triggers, and responsiveness to discipline. At times, it will take experimentation to discover which of the 16.6 million Googled ideas will best shape your child for the future, but the art of discipline allows opportunity to creatively design an approach that fits both you

Tips to Make Discipline More Effective

- Be aware of your child's abilities and limitations. Children develop at different rates and have different strengths and weaknesses. When your child misbehaves, it may be that he simply cannot do what you are asking of him or he does not understand what you are asking.
- Think before you speak. Once you make a rule or promise, you will need to stick to it. Be sure you are being realistic. Think if it is really necessary before saying "no."
- Remember that children do what "works." If your child throws a temper tantrum in the grocery store and you bribe him to stop by giving him candy, he will probably throw another tantrum the next time you go. Make an effort to avoid reinforcing the wrong kinds of behavior, even with just your attention.
- Work toward consistency. No one is consistent all of the time. But try to make sure that your goals, rules, and approaches to discipline stay the same from day to day. Children find frequent changes confusing and often resort to testing limits just to find out what the limits are.
- Pay attention to your child's feelings. If you can figure out why your child is misbehaving, you are one step closer to solving the problem. It is kinder and helps with cooperation when you let your child know that you understand. For example, "I know you are feeling sad that your friend is leaving, but you still have to pick up your toys."
- Learn to see mistakes—including your own—as opportunities to learn. If you do not handle a situation well the first time, don't despair. Think about what you could have done differently, and try to do it the next time. If you feel you have made a real mistake in the heat of the moment, wait to cool down, apologize to your child, and explain how you will handle the situation in the future. Be sure to keep your promise. This gives your child a good model of how to recover from mistakes.[16]

and your child. The American Academy of Pediatrics provides great principles to shape our approach.

Actions speak louder than words. Over the years, moms from many cultures have lived by (and taught their children) this little phrase. If we want truthful children, they need to hear us tell the truth. Even to telemarketers calling at dinnertime. If we want kids who share, they need to see us share. Even if it means giving up our morning mocha. If we want kids who clean their rooms, we're more likely to see results if we keep a tidy room. (The theory may break down a bit with this one, but I'm hopeful my kids come around by the time they become parents.) This doesn't mean moms must be perfect all the time or risk ruining their children. Watching how we handle our mistakes shapes how our children handle their mistakes. "Mommy should have stayed within the speed limit. Now she has to tell the nice policeman she's sorry."

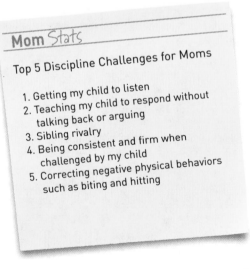

Mom Stats

Top 5 Discipline Challenges for Moms

1. Getting my child to listen
2. Teaching my child to respond without talking back or arguing
3. Sibling rivalry
4. Being consistent and firm when challenged by my child
5. Correcting negative physical behaviors such as biting and hitting

FIELD STUDY

Squelching Sibling Squabbling

"It's my turn to pick the movie," Brita hollered at her younger sister.

"Nooo, it's my turn," Johanna bellowed back.

Here we go again, I thought.

"Mom," Brita whined to me, "it's my turn, remember? Johanna picked the movie yesterday."

"No, I don't remember," I snapped at her, "and I can't deal with this right now. I have to feed the twins."

This constant arguing over whose turn it was between my girls, ages 2 and 3½, was driving me crazy. Because my infant twins demanded so much attention, I really didn't have time to keep complicated charts and graphs. But something had to be done to squelch the bickering.

That afternoon I walked by a kitchen gadget store in our local mall and saw the little magnet you put on the dishwasher that says "clean" on one side and "dirty" on the other. *Aha!*

When I got home I printed both girls' names out, laminated them, and then pasted one on each side of a refrigerator magnet. That day I started flipping the magnet to keep track of whose turn it was for just about everything. And it really worked—if I was good at remembering to flip it. This also took the "me" out of the argument; if the girls asked me whose turn it was for something I would remind them to look at the fridge to find their answer.

—Corynn, mom of four

Practicum

* My top five challenges to discipline are . . .
* To shape my child for the future, I'm willing to face these challenges head-on by . . .
* Share your top discipline challenges at mom-ology.org. Ⓜ

2.4 Finesse Requires Patience, Perspective, and Prayer

At the start of part two, I shared a study in which 54 percent of parents stated they feel successful most days. Most days. But what about the days that don't fit into the "most days" category, when success is elusive? The days when it is increasingly apparent Baby is speech and gross motor skills delayed. The days we realize our poor eating or spending or media habits are having a negative impact on our kids but feel too overwhelmed to make a change. The days the school calls for a conference because our preschooler is lying or bullying or too hyperactive in class. The days we huddle under the covers, hesitant to get out of bed for fear we'll lose it again over an unpaid bill, a lost little sandal, or rice cereal and grape juice glopped on the kitchen floor. How does a mom finesse those days?

If you've never experienced those days, feel free to skip right over to the next section on mom relationships.

On second thought, before you move on, note the location of these paragraphs. You're likely to need them at some point.

Shaping children is nonstop challenging. To borrow from a popular Christmas song, kids "see you when you're sleeping," "know when you're awake," "know when you've been bad or good"—so there's bound to be mistakes! We need to watch out, but we don't need to be perfect. How we finesse mistakes, overcome problems, and figure out what to erase and redo will shape our children, too.

Children have minds of their own, the ability to make choices. At times, those choices will bring great pain, causing us to question our mothering finesse. I think that's one reason I love the story of the prodigal son so much. The boy makes horrible choices, defying the values he'd been raised with, but when he gets to the end of his own resources, he returns home. Proverbs 22:6 explains this prodigal phenomenon like this: "Train a child in the way he should go, and when he is old he will not turn from it." What we illustrate for our kids today sticks with them for a lifetime.

Patience. Today you may not see results, but you will.

Patience. Today you may have made a mom mistake. Forgive yourself and go for a redo.

Keep a long-term perspective. A work of art isn't shaped in a day. Michelangelo's great masterpiece, the ceiling of the Sistine Chapel, took four years to create (and he had assistants). During that time, Michelangelo dealt with mold, poverty, a contorted body, diminished vision, altered eating habits, and perpetual tiredness. Sound familiar, Mom?

Despite the challenges, Michelangelo persevered and for five hundred years his beautiful work has graced the Sistine Chapel and brought glory to God. When you feel like a moldy, impoverished, blind, hungry, tired mom, close your eyes and envision the finished masterpiece once again. Remember what you are working toward.

And pray. God is listening and he cares deeply about you and your child. Whether you're feeling successful or success seems elusive, take a minute each morning before your feet hit the ground running to ask for patience and perspective, wisdom and strength. Snatch a second while chopping the pear pieces for snack and ask God for peace and the right words to comfort a whiny toddler at the pediatrician. Reflect as your head hits the pillow each night and ask for finesse to artfully shape the masterpiece entrusted into your care.

 Practicum

* I'm struggling as a mom because . . .
* As my child watches me work through this struggle, I want her to learn . . .
* The best thing about my mom finesse is . . .
* Write a short prayer, expressing both your struggles and strengths as a mom. Ask God for the finesse to handle both as you shape your child.
* Share about your mom finesse triumphs and struggles at mom-ology.org. M

Quick Review

Mothers feel successful most—but not all—of the time.

- Mothering requires patience with myself and my child.
- Keep a long-term perspective; shaping a masterpiece takes time.
- Pray during the successful days and also the not-so-successful days. God gives finesse.

Living together is an art.
—William Pickens

PART THREE

CIRCLE

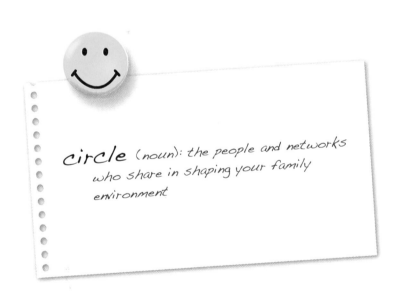

circle (noun): the people and networks who share in shaping your family environment

3.1 Community Circle

3.1.1 Antidote to Isolation

Between dropping off my children at school and arriving at work one morning, I was engulfed in a wave of loneliness. Having always lived in the same area, encircled by long-established relationships, I was unprepared for the isolation I experienced after moving to a new state. Before moving, taking kids to and from school was a community experience involving carpool friends and chatting up other moms in driveways or the school parking lot. I knew all the moms and teachers and they knew me and my kids. Since the move, all the driving was up to me and I didn't recognize one other person in the drop-off area. When I was done crying I rubbed the streaky mascara lines from under my eyes and pasted on a smile, determined to deal with my loneliness all by myself.

Does anyone else see the irony in that? Loneliness is probably the last thing we can deal with by ourselves. But, embarrassed by my need, I didn't want anyone else to know.

Like moving, motherhood brings changes to our relationships with extended family and dear friends and, if we're married, changes to the relationship we have with our husband. Even our outer circle of relationships, those people we interact with occasionally such as health care professionals and the kid who bags our groceries, change when we become moms. And sometimes, in the midst of intensely bonding with one little human being, we feel very isolated from the rest of the world. Yet another irony many of us are embarrassed to talk about.

A plethora of research supports the value of surrounding moms and their families with strong relationships. According to Promoting Healthy Families research, relationships are one of five protective factors that prevent child abuse and neglect. "Trusted and caring family and friends provide emotional support to parents by offering encouragement and assistance in facing daily challenges."[1] In her book based on research conducted by the Search Institute, author, parent educator, and mother of two Jolene Roehlkepartain writes:

> The stress and intensity of parenting a preschooler is the reason why your adult relationships are so important. You need supportive adults around you. You need strong friendships, even if you don't have a lot of time to spend with those friends. Your adult relationships can make your life as a parent much easier and also make your life more personally meaningful.[2]

As moms, supportive relationships are not only important during the preschool years but throughout all our children's ages and stages. When asked why relationships were important, parents involved in the Building Strong Families study responded they value

- people telling them they're doing a good job as a parent;
- talking with other parents about parenting issues;
- getting parenting advice from trusted professionals;
- people they trust—including friends, neighbors, and extended family—spending more positive time with their kids.[3]

A circle of people and networks can share in shaping a family's environment, making it easier for moms to navigate the joys and challenges of mothering. Within that circle, a variety of relationships provides an antidote for isolation and loneliness. Raising kids within these relationships provides a safe place to live, love, and belong, an authentic community where moms and families can develop their strengths and work through their challenges. Moms shared that they find this community in a variety of places.

 Practicum

* As a mom, I can tell my relationships have changed by . . .
* I look for authentic community at . . .
* What do you most want to find within this community?
* Share what you're looking for in a community at mom-ology.org. Ⓜ

3.1.2 Circle Essentials: Time and Trust

Eventually, I let a few people in on my loneliness and began building new relationships. Unlike chocolate pudding and oatmeal, there's no instant version! Along the way, I developed a great appreciation for military moms who face the changing relationship challenge on a regular basis. Holly, a military mom of two, shares this story.

Mom Stats

My family is engaged in community through . . .

Extended family: 55%
Neighbors: 53%
School/playgroup: 71%
Work: 34%
Spiritual community: 76%

FIELD STUDY

Creating Family

The phone was always ringing during our four years in North Carolina. Almost as soon as we were stationed there, I began making friends. There wasn't much to do around the base, and with Phil, my husband, deployed much of the time, I needed people to fill the empty spaces. I found a MOPS group, became involved in a church, and began to "create family" for myself and my two young children. Soon, when I took my daughter to preschool in the morning, I knew at least half of the moms, really knew them.

Our current assignment in Florida is much different. We moved over a year ago, and yet my phone rarely rings. When it does ring, it's usually my husband. I'm still a people lover, so what's different this time? I think one difference is that my need for friends isn't as great. Phil rarely travels away from home and has predictable work hours, so I spend more time with him. This is priority number one for me as I'm the product of military parents who divorced. I don't want that for my kids!

The many fun things to do in our new location keep us very busy. That's good and bad. Good because we enjoy these as a family, bad because the stuff to do distracts us from being with other families. It's hard to find time. Time plays another role in this relationship-building desert I'm currently in. Since I know we're not going to live here very long, I wonder if it's really worth investing time in relationships, knowing how much it will hurt when we have to say good-bye. I know it will happen; friends do disappear.

When we moved here, I was excited because we'd again be living close to a couple we counted among our "bestest friends." But the friendship we experienced in the past didn't reappear; as a matter of fact, it has all but disappeared. I feel betrayed and hurt. I also tried building a friendship with another mom when we first moved, but she shared some of our personal conversations with others. Again, betrayed! I have to admit that time and a lack of trust are influencing my current decisions about relationship building.

Maybe my phone will soon start ringing a little more often. I'm getting to know another mom and see some strong friend potential in her. And last weekend at church I volunteered in a different area and met some new people I liked. I'm hoping that by investing some time in these new relationships and bravely pushing past my fear of betrayal, I'll begin to "create family" for my immediate family once again.

—Holly, mom of two

Investing in her closest human relationship, the one with her husband, is a high priority. But Holly is currently struggling with the next ring of relationships, her friends. Two factors are essential to the development of these critical relationships, the same two factors I've heard other mom friends share: time and trust.

Time is essential to building relationships. You have to spend time to develop a friendship—to notice another person, chat with her, share experiences, discover her interests, and find ways to meet her needs. Isn't it interesting how we define this as "spending" time? Clearly we understand that relationships have a cost, a value. Is the value you place on relationships reflected by how much time you spend in developing them? I'm quite sure that is not always true in my case. Like Holly, at times I find that doing stuff, even good stuff, steals time away from being in relationships. We need to consider our time-spending habits often, adjusting them to ensure we're investing enough in relationships.

As Holly continues to meet her potential friend for coffee or sessions at the gym, she'll have opportunities to create meaningful connections. Those connections will become part of their shared history. Holly is also wisely using this time of close proximity to her husband, Phil, to build their relationship.

Trust is even more essential to building relationships than time. Holly fears betrayal and the pain of loss. Those are valid fears that are shared by many, and they make trust difficult. I fear something different. My fear is trusting people with my less-than-perfect, messy self. My fear of rejection was at the core of my decision to hide the signs of loneliness from other people.

Whether it stems from betrayal, loss, or rejection, fear sometimes keeps us from opening the door of our lives to other people. Instead of welcoming new relationships, we treat them like the big, bad wolf. We build invasion-resistant walls using bricks of superficial conversation and seemingly safe activities, but we leave ourselves isolated and alone. Trust involves vulnerably sharing our struggles and mistakes, our insecurities and questions. Trust also involves holding shared stuff in confidence. Had Holly been able to trust the first woman she attempted to build a friendship with when she moved, the relationship might have grown, benefiting both women.

Mom Stats

I have at least one "safe" person to talk to.

Yes: 96%
No: 4%

Mom Stats

In relationships, trust is developed by—

- Keeping promises
- Keeping a confidence
- Offering sincere compliments
- Listening attentively
- Overlooking a fault
- Tactfully addressing a fault when needed
- Respecting differences
- Acting honestly
- Acceptance

- Time
- Working through challenges successfully
- Shared projects

 Practicum

* My relationships are strong when I "spend" time . . .
* My greatest fear in relationships is . . .
* What would it take for you to replace that fear with trust? M

3.1.3 Rings around the Family

How many friends will you have in a lifetime? Searching online, I discovered answers ranging from two to over a billion! I think we can safely say most of us fall somewhere in between. Part of the reason for such wildly varied answers is that respondents struggled to define and categorize their relationships. For clarity as you read and consider your relationships, here are the definitions I'm using.

acquaintances: people one knows slightly or casually (neighbors; people at playgroup, school, gym, work, social activities, school, or online; health care personnel; and service providers such as dry cleaner, mechanic, and librarian)

family and friends: extended family (parents, in-laws, siblings, cousins, aunts, uncles) and friends (people with whom you share a strong mutual affection)

immediate family: husband or parenting partner, children

The following diagram of concentric circles helps define the significance of the people and networks who share in shaping our family environments. Of course, people don't always fit into nice little categories, and at different times some will move between rings. Sometimes that's a happy migration. When I met my husband, Bruce, during the first week of a college chemistry class, he was in my outer ring of acquaintances. By the second week of class, he migrated (maybe I should say leapt?) into the middle ring, and for more than two decades he's been my much-appreciated partner in the inner circle.

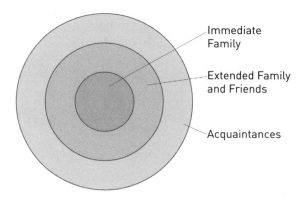

Immediate Family

Extended Family and Friends

Acquaintances

During a season of change, like when we enter motherhood, our relationships often migrate. Friends may move to the outer ring as interests and schedules change. An acquaintance, especially if she's a mom, may migrate into the middle ring. As we talked about earlier, new people, people we connect with because of our child or because we share the common bond of mothering, may also enter our circle. Some people, a beloved babysitter for instance, may hover between all three rings, depending on her relationship with your family.

In the midst of mothering, it's easy to let cultivating relationships drop to the bottom of the to-do list. When combined, the relationships from each ring of your circle offer opportunities for a wide variety of support. However, a 2002 survey revealed that 53 percent of parents don't utilize many of those relationship resources. That statistic surprised and saddened me. The people in our circle provide practical help, a sense of belonging, an increased sense of self-worth, and a feeling of security. I hope you're a part of the 47 percent who do allow others to support you and your family.[4]

 Practicum

* Write the initials for as many people as you can think of in the diagram on page 140.
* Circle the initials of people you are most likely to turn to for support.
* Are there any gaps that need to be filled?

 Quick Review

The people in your circle of relationships form a support network for your family.

* Raising kids in authentic community is an antidote for isolation and loneliness.
* Time and trust are essential for developing relationships.
* Our circle is made up of three rings: immediate family, extended family and friends, and acquaintances.

3.2 Acquaintances: The Outer Ring

Have you ever felt disconnected during a day filled with people? You've jogged side-by-side with strangers in the park, talked by cell phone about completing a project, met with the playgroup, and waited in line at the ATM with twelve other people, all while participating in a day-long conversation with your preschooler about flashlights—and felt alone. In the midst of so much doing, sometimes we forget about beings. Human beings. The people we interact with throughout any given day aren't just waiting to be crossed off the to-do list of our lives. Many of them would welcome a connection, creating an occasion to know and be known.

3.2.1 Neighbors

Everyone should get to know their neighbors . . . you never know when you will need someone you trust to lean on.

—Blog post from Fargo resident after the floods of 2009

Other than our immediate family, the people we live in closest proximity with may be people we don't know very well. At least if you're like the majority of people. A Halifax, Massachusetts, newspaper article shared survey results from the question, "How well do you know your neighbors?"

Very well: 0%
We're pretty friendly: 42%
We barely know each other: 41%
Have never met: 17%[5]

Do those results surprise you? How do relationships in your neighborhood compare? Good neighbors can sign for packages, keep an eye out for problems, share a shovel or snowblower after a storm, and help look for runaway dogs and cats. They can share in daily life. In a world where we often know more about what's happening halfway around the world than we know about the people with whom we share a common wall, how do we get better acquainted with the people next door?

FIELD STUDY

Just Jump the Fence

I love the idea of connecting with neighbors and creating community, but it can feel daunting when we ruin it with our expectations. I'm definitely guilty of falling into the "perfect" trap and feeling overwhelmed at the idea of an impromptu gathering at our house.

Luckily, a few of my neighbors shared my fear. So we banded together to overcome the "expectations monster." Now, when one family in our neighborhood suggests having dinner together, we set a time and then jump the fence into their yard. We also set the following ground rules:

- No spending. Raid the fridge and pantry for food and drink on hand.
- No serving dishes. Leave the pretty bowls and fancy napkins at home.
- No grooming the children before coming over.

We've found other ways to meet our neighbors, something as simple as grabbing a baggie of change and filling paper cups with lemonade. Let your kids be the icebreakers as they camp out on your sidewalk waving signs at passing cars and unsuspecting dog-walkers. We've met some amazing families through our lemonade stands! Of course, homemade cookies and brownies also create very loyal customers.

We also frequently play in the front yard. A ten-dollar Slip 'n Slide does the trick when it comes to entertaining kids. Place it in your front yard and the kiddos come running. Set up a few lawn chairs on the driveway for the grown-ups.

Give it a try like we did. Just jump the fence, hot dog buns and chips in hand, and gather at the nearest grill. Keep expectations and costs low, and you'll discover the beauty of building community in your own neighborhood.

—Merideth, mom of two

Simple ways to meet the neighbors

- Sit on your front porch or landing
- Attend a neighborhood meeting
- Walk the block
- Work outside
- Deliver cookies
- Borrow a cup of sugar

Practicum

* How well do you know your neighbors?
  Participate in our survey at mom-ology.org.

3.2.2 Skin-on Groups

> My story is the story of so many moms in my group. We all wanted a place to be with other moms like us. We wanted to feel part of a group. I didn't have any mom friends and I felt overwhelmed by the relief and acceptance and safety when I walked into my first meeting. I knew I had found the place where I would grow and become a better mom. Over the last three years it has been 100% great!
>
> —Anonymous response to MOPS annual group survey

One of the best decisions I ever made was to accept a friend's invitation to join a mom's group. My initial response was no. It sounded kind of boring to sit around and discuss housework, potty training, and how to make organic baby food. Although those topics did come up (and I learned some new ideas!), the group was so much more than that. We swapped babysitting and baby stuff, talked and listened without passing judgment, discovered new things about ourselves and mothering, laughed and cried together, and continued making room for more moms. Several of the moms in my group became close friends.

Joining a group, whether it's a mom's group, a playgroup of moms and kids, a fitness class, a book club, or another type of group, provides a chance to meet new people, explore new ideas and activities, participate in a cause, or simply relax and have fun.

Intimidated at the thought of meeting a group of strangers? One thing that can help is realizing that it is very likely that other moms in the group share your fears. Don't just stand around waiting for someone to say hi. They are all just as scared as you are. Introduce yourself and try to find something you have in common to talk about.

Mom Stats

I'm involved with a group of moms.

Yes: 87%
No: 13%

Participate in our survey at mom-ology.org. [M]

Look for a group that matches your interests and priorities. In her book *Life on Planet Mom*, Lisa Bergren offers a list of things to consider.[6]

- Emotional health
- Mental growth
- Social connections
- Health/exercise
- Faith
- Balance
- Politics
- Marriage
- Family Life
- Friendship

Participating in a group expands a mom's opportunities to build relationships, moving her from isolation to a sense of connection and security. Find some mothers you can talk to, hang out with, and call on when you need help. And when you find a group you like, be on the lookout for another mom to invite. You'll be doing both of you a favor, and your kids will benefit, too.

I was invited to my group by my new neighbor. Having moved to this community from out of state, I was really missing a strong support network of women that I knew I needed. Through my group, I met many of the women I consider friends today, and I grew into a leader (didn't see that one coming!). I have gone from the lonely mom at the playground to the happy-go-lucky and often quirky leader of my group. I am having a wonderful time encouraging other mothers to get involved.

—Anonymous response to MOPS annual group survey

Mom Stats

Groups Moms Love

Where can you find a group that matches your priorities? Moms in our survey shared some of the groups they've found. Having been involved in MOPS for so many years, I hope you'll check our website for a group near you (www.MOPS.org).

MOPS (Mothers of Preschoolers)
MOMSnext (Moms of School-Age Kids)
Mothers of Multiples

Adoption/foster support group
Playgroup
Single parents group
Scrapbooking buddies
YWCA or YMCA
Bible study
Book club
Homeschooling
Special Education PTSA (Parent Teacher Student Assoc.)
Moms in Touch
Breastfeeding group

Moms Club, Intl
Mums and Tots
Bunco group
Fitness class
Coffee group
PTO (Parent Teacher Organization)

Practicum

* What I would most want to find in a mom's group is . . .
* The mom I could invite to join a group is . . .
* The kind of group I would most like to join . . .

3.2.3 Mommy Wars!

Believe it or not, when you join a mom group other moms may not all share your decisions and opinions about raising kids. Really! About the only place I know of where there are more opinions on mothering than a mom's group is the internet. How moms handle those differences can make or break a mom's group. Originally coined in the late 1980s by *Child* magazine to describe the tension that existed between working and stay-at-home moms, the term "mommy wars" has extended to cover a vast number of mommy differences.

Breast or bottle? Cloth or disposable? City or suburbs? Crib or family bed? Home school or day school? Vaccine or no vaccine? Sling or swing? Why do the differences in how we choose to raise our kids turn otherwise sane mamas into snarky antagonists? Mollie Ziegler Hemingway, mother of two, offers her take in a recent article on the subject: "Much of the hype comes from the all-consuming nature of motherhood, causing sleep-deprived and overworked moms to focus on childrearing to the point that crazy fights seem entirely normal. And, much of the angst reflects our fear that if other parents do things differently, they will pass judgment on the decisions we've made."[7]

Online Mom Groups

Facebook, Twitter, Nesting, YouTube, LinkedIn, Meetup, mom blogs, and forums all provide opportunities to build relationships with other moms. Compared to skin-on mom groups, they have advantages and disadvantages. Participate in both and get the best of both worlds.

Advantages
- 24/7 access to advice and information
- Easy to make friends
- Meet a wide variety of women
- Easy to find a group that matches your specific needs and interests
- Can chat during naptime and when the kids are sick

Disadvantages
- Easier to misrepresent yourself
- You don't actually know who you are talking to
- Gobbles time
- No body language to help interpret dialogue
- Can't provide an actual shoulder to cry on or big mama bear hug

Ouch! I see another relationship fear at the bottom of our battle positions. Is it possible that if we are each uniquely designed to mother our uniquely designed children, then we *should* have uniquely designed approaches to raising them? Truly, there are certain standards of health and safety we want to see as part of every child's upbringing, but that still leaves room for many approaches. Hemingway closes her article by saying, "Just as we wouldn't rearrange colleagues' offices or tinker with their computers, neither should we presume to know best how they should manage their families."[8] After almost three decades, don't you think its time to put an end to the mommy wars? Let's agree to embrace our own approaches to mothering and graciously allow other moms to do the same.

FIELD STUDY

To Share or Not to Share?

My eighteen-month-old daughter, Glory, walked over to another toddler in our playgroup and started to grab a yellow building block out of the little girl's hand. The little girl held on tightly, twisted away from Glory, and said, "Mine."

The girl's mother, Sarah, and I were sitting next to each other on the floor nearby and both saw this interaction. We were just getting to know each other.

"Lizzie," the mom scooted near to her daughter and touched her shoulder to get her attention. "Share. Don't you want to give this block to Glory?" The little girl emphatically shook her head no and held the block tightly to her chest.

"It's okay," I interjected. "Glory shouldn't be able to just walk up and take the block away from her."

"But sharing is something we're working on," said Sarah.

I wondered if I should say what I was thinking and decided it was important for me to be honest. I was learning to be confident in my mothering decisions. I didn't know how Sarah was going to react but felt I needed to say something. "I think sharing is important, but my child needs to learn how to be patient and wait. I don't think it is right for her to walk up and try to grab the block away from your daughter."

Sarah laughed nervously and we dropped the subject. She didn't force Lizzie to give Glory the block after I said this but I wondered if I'd offended her.

—Joy, mom of two

VOICES

The biggest mom conflict I've been involved in has been around the topic of . . .

Whether or not to celebrate fictional representations of holidays (e.g., Easter Bunny, Santa Claus).

—Kristin, mom of four

Early potty training!

—Pam, mom of three

That we homeschool and practice attached parenting.

—Megan, mom of four

Whether to medicate my child who has ADHD.

—Amy, mom of two

> About raising my kids bilingual.
>
> —Anja, mom of two

 Practicum

* When I have a different opinion from other moms, I most often . . .
* I can express my opinion without engaging in warfare by . . . Ⓜ

3.2.4 Care and Service Providers

I still remember the tall, well-dressed salesman who for several years helped fit my oldest daughter with shoes. Her feet were long, thin, and high-arched. They also grew faster than my shoe budget. During our initial foray into fitting out-of-the-norm-sized feet, he took the time to discover my daughter's favorite colors and my price range. I took the time to memorize his name and work schedule. I know he probably wrote down our information in a little book somewhere, but each time he remembered our names or called when a certain brand we liked went on sale, I felt valued.

In many practical ways, care and service providers support moms, influencing our kids through the way they handle their jobs. Some of them we interact with only once or twice, some on an ongoing basis over long periods of time, and others, like teachers and care providers, on an almost daily basis. The closer and more frequent the interaction, the more important it is to develop positive, ongoing relationships. Fortunately, all that's required in most cases is common sense and good manners.

Know and be known. Whether it's a pediatric surgeon or a child care provider, this is the foundation for success in these relationships. Know the person providing the service, their name, credentials, experience, and whenever possible some personal information. I know my son's pediatrician works with teens at his church and likes antique cars and skiing. I also know he completed his pediatric internship and residency at the University of Texas. Besides knowing his medical information, Dr. K. knows my son likes fast cars, struggles with math, and wants to be a Marine. Knowing and being known improves the quality of our relationship and ensures excellent care for my son.

Share values and choices. As often as possible, select people who share your values and choices in parenting. One of my friends switched nurse-practitioners when she discovered the provider had a low opinion of homeopathic remedies. A child caregiver who adheres to the philosophy that children should be left to "cry it out" probably isn't the best choice for a mom committed to attachment parenting. You probably won't find someone exactly like you, but try to find a match in the areas that matter most.

Clarify expectations. Especially when working with care providers, clearly state your expectations before committing. Schedules, method of communication, parenting philosophies, meals, payment, and other factors should be understood before hiring. Besides clearly stating your expectations, take time to ask the provider to share hers.

Be respectful. Honor the person's time, expertise, and willingness to provide a service to your family. If you've chosen a provider you believe has appropriate expertise, then assume her opinions, advice, and service are based on what she knows is best. She may not be the vast information well of the internet, but she does know her field and she can provide a more personalized response to your child's need.

Communicate regularly. Share information that impacts emotional and physical health. Let the provider know of any changes in your family or child. Ask about the provider's own situation, especially if they are offering in-home care. If an issue comes up, take it calmly and directly to the provider.

Show appreciation. A heartfelt thank you, a birthday card, or a holiday gift in appropriate situations, shows gratitude for good service. When applicable, refer friends. New business is always appreciated.

Pay promptly. Your financial problems should not become their financial problems. If payment will be late, let the provider know as soon as possible and don't quibble about payment policies and late fees.

 Practicum

* Who are the service providers most involved in your child's life?
* How can you develop a relationship that enhances your child's well-being? M

Quick Review

The outer ring of relationships encircles the family with support and a sense of belonging.

- Get to know your neighbors.
- Mom groups can be an antidote to loneliness.
- Avoid mommy wars by respecting other approaches to raising kids.
- Healthy relationships with service providers improve the quality of care our children receive.

3.3 Friends and Extended Family: The Middle Ring

3.3.1 Friends

Nearly three-quarters of moms surveyed saw a change in their friendships after becoming moms.[9] When our bodies, brains, and day planners all begin revolving around a new little being, and we're trying to figure out not only who they are but who we are, we're looking for a friend who can respond, "No way. Me, too!" Unless our pre-mom friends are having kids at the same time we are, they just can't fill that role. That doesn't mean you won't still be friends; it does mean your friendship needs have expanded.

If what's being posted on mom blogs is any indication, getting beyond the smile and wave stage and finding deep friendship is scary. When you think about it, it's not unlike another scary life stage we all went through. What does this remind you of? We're buying bigger bras, hormones are haywire, we've moved into a new scene, and it seems like everyone else is more together than we are. We check out each other's accessories—"Ohhh! She's wearing an Ergo carrier and her Jujube diaper tote is just too cute." Yep, you guessed it, junior high all over again.

Hopefully, we've picked up a few relational skills since then. Like how to be less judgmental. Discussing the topic of finding friends, one mom posted, "I finally learned to mentally slap some duct tape over my judgmental mouth when I'm with a group of moms and focus on what we have in common." Sound advice.

We've learned it's worth the risk to make the first move: "Hi, I'm Michele and this is Toby. How old's your little guy?" Several moms recommended printing calling or business cards (free or low cost ones are available at www.vistaprint.com) to share when they meet a potential mom friend. Don't worry about looking needy; other moms will appreciate not having to handle the gum wrapper or dried up baby wipe with your phone number written in crayon. Although to a mom looking for a friend, those crumpled scraps may seem like pure gold.

Having passed through the junior high years, experience has also taught us that most often friendship takes time. We may not recognize what Anne of Green Gables called, "A bosom friend—an intimate friend, you know—a really kindred spirit to whom I can confide my inmost soul" over just one latte or a single playdate. Let's all say it together: "Friendship takes time." Doing things together such as exercising, scrapbooking, or volunteering provides an opportunity to connect repeatedly. If a friendship doesn't work out, you've at least done something good for yourself.

Volunteering has led to some of my deepest friendships. There's something about working together toward a common cause, investing in something beyond oneself, that unites people.

That's especially true when we volunteer together on a regular basis.

Besides companionship, friendships offer numerous health benefits.

- Increase your sense of belonging and purpose
- Boost your happiness
- Reduce stress
- Improve your self-worth
- Decrease your risk of serious mental illness
- Help you weather traumas, such as divorce, illness, job loss, or death of a loved one
- Encourage you to change unhealthy lifestyle habits, such as excessive drinking or lack of exercise

In their book *The Power of a Positive Friend*, Karol Ladd and Terry Ann Kelly share an anonymous email that contains the essence of girlfriends.

I sat under a tree in the hot sun on a summer day, drinking iced tea and getting to know my new sister-in-law. Not much older than I, but already the mother of three, she seemed to me to be experienced and wise. "Get yourself some girlfriends," she advised, clinking the ice cubes in her glass. "You are going to need girlfriends. Go places with them; do things with them."

"What a funny piece of advice," I thought. Hadn't I just gotten married? I was a married woman for goodness' sake, not a young girl who needed girlfriends. But I listened to this new sister-in-law. I got myself some girlfriends. And as the years tumbled by, one after another, gradually I came to understand that she knew what she was talking about. Here's what I know about girlfriends:

- Girlfriends bring casseroles and scrub your bathroom when you are sick.
- Girlfriends keep your children and keep your secrets.
- Girlfriends don't always tell you that you're right, but they're usually honest.
- Girlfriends still love you, even when they don't agree with your choices.
- Girlfriends laugh with you, and you don't need canned jokes to start the laughter.
- Girlfriends pull you out of jams.
- Girlfriends are there for you, in an instant and truly, when the hard times come.
- Girlfriends listen when you lose a job or a husband.
- My girlfriends bless my life. Once we were young, with no idea of the incredible joys or the incredible sorrows that lay ahead. Nor did we know how much we would need each other.[10]

Do you have any girlfriend definitions to add? Post them at mom-ology.org.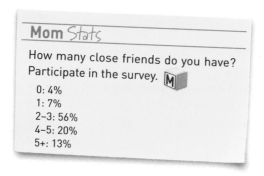

Mom Stats

How many close friends do you have? Participate in the survey.

    0: 4%
    1: 7%
    2–3: 56%
    4–5: 20%
    5+: 13%

Practicum

* Friendships improve my life by . . .
* How many friends do you think you need?
* If you feel the need for more friends, what kind of friend are you looking for? **[M]**

Mentors

About 36 percent of moms in our survey had a mentor. In the mom world, mentoring is usually an informal relationship with a mom who is farther down the road in her mothering journey. Mentors provide perspective, a listening ear, encouragement, and wisdom. In my mind one of the best things my mentors have done is to pray for me and my family. Great mentors are willing to share their strengths and weaknesses. Sometimes mom, mother-in-law, or sister fulfills this role. If not (or in addition to), be on the lookout for someone with qualities such as honesty and humor whom you admire and feel a connection with. When you meet someone like this, be bold and ask her to be a part of your life. And remember, after you've been mothering for a short while, a newer mom may ask you to be her mentor. Consider saying yes!

3.3.2 Extended Family

My oldest claimed the title "first grandchild" on all sides of the family and "first great-grandchild" on my husband's side. We were a popular trio! The first hint of trouble didn't come until baby's first Christmas. Bruce's family has . . . well, let's just say, some interesting dynamics. His parents had divorced and both remarried before he was three. By the time we were married, Bruce's mom and stepdad had passed away and relationships between his dad, stepmom, and the rest of his family were strained. We were very close to both his grandmothers though. Coming from a relatively stable extended family, I wasn't used to navigating relational mine fields or eating Christmas dinner at quite so many places. Traveling to all the grandmothers' houses frayed my nerves and left almost no time for us to be family. It was a miserable Christmas.

My mom was the best, offering great schedule flexibility the next year. She said she remembered what it felt like and advised that I work something out with Bruce's side of the family as well. I should have clued in on her wisdom right then. Alas, I was kind of a "know it all" first-time mom, too confident for my own good, and we continued making the rounds a second Christmas. We had a second miserable Christmas.

By the third Christmas, my mom was starting to look a whole lot wiser and we invited everyone to our house for Christmas. And made it a potluck. Christmas went back to being a celebration.

Holidays are just part of the extended family dynamics that need reworking when kids arrive. There's how to handle unsolicited advice and differences of opinion. Or figuring out what to do with family members whose life choices and habits might be harmful. One mom I know worried about how to manage her alcoholic father.

How do you explain why Junior can't ride in the car with Grandpa? Ever. What if your mother and mother-in-law have a bad case of grandma rivalry, each trying to outdo the other in gifts of love?

Love. In the midst of all the tough stuff, the love extended family offers has immeasurable value and it's offered in many different ways. My sister-in-law expresses love in carefully selected gifts and handmade cards. My kids spent weeks putting together a slide show for my parents' anniversary celebration. They had no trouble finding pictures of themselves with Grandma and Grandpa because my parents have taken them to so many great places. That's one way my parents show love. Most of the time, family members via marriage and the original group you were born into offer a rich resource of love for your kids. Every family has challenges, but working through them is worth the time and effort. How to make that happen?

- Set realistic expectations. Your family is not a bunch of actors reciting the lines of your script. They are people with strengths and weaknesses just like you, often with scripts of their own.
- Figure out what you need, prioritize what's most important, and communicate your priorities firmly and graciously.
- Appreciate the good. No family is perfect.
- Be respectful, even when you don't agree.
- Identify family hot buttons and avoid them as much as possible.
- Keep your sense of humor.
- Forgive.
- Love on them. Open your heart and home.

FIELD STUDY

The In-Laws

"Charles, after your parents leave from visiting us, I feel so exhausted. I know they come to help us, but they go nonstop and constantly want to do stuff with us. It keeps me busy keeping them busy. And we didn't even get a night out to ourselves," I complained to my husband.

"I know. I'm sorry, Babe, they mean well. You just have to be more direct with them. They can't read your mind. If we want a date while they're here next time, we'll put it on their schedule and let them know that's what we want. They'll understand, they just need to be told," Charles tried to explain, but it's so hard for me to relate to his parents because they are so different from mine.

When my parents visit they offer to stay at a hotel to give us some space, whereas Charles's family insists on staying with us, in our three-bedroom, one bathroom, 1,200-square-foot home. They strongly believe family should always stay together. I appreciate that they're happy to make a fort out of blankets and sleep with the kids on the floor, but it's just a little too much "together" for me.

I've also found my mom and Charles's mom have very different personalities. My mom is very emotional and intuitive, she knows what I need and I don't have to tell her. She'll sense that I need to go somewhere to be alone and just read a book—rest and not accomplish anything. Charles's mom is more productive and resourceful. Give her a list and she'll get it done.

Both sets of grandparents adore our children, but they interact with them very differently. For example, my parents will take the kids to the park and play for hours, while my in-laws will take them to the zoo and then out to eat, more of a planned event. Either way they're all about loving and getting to know our kids, for which I'm beyond grateful.

Over the years, I've learned to accept the differences between our families, but at times it's still hard for me to be direct with my in-laws. I feel like I'm ordering them around, giving out lists of tasks to be done. I feel a bit demanding when I give them specific times and dates for when Charles and I would like some alone time, but they prefer this.

Rather than expecting my in-laws to be more like my family, I've learned to respect their ways. They definitely love us, and I love that.

—Tracy, mom of two

VOICES

To build relationships with extended family I . . .

Constantly entertain!! Our door is always open and our kids are right there in the mix.

—Augusta, mom of three

Try to be available to my husband's siblings by exchanging child care with them. We take turns hosting the group for dinner each month.

—Jan, mom of three

Email and use Facebook to stay connected since we all live in different states.

—Kelly, mom of three

Keep a family blog.

—Vanessa, mom of one

Let them have time with my children away from me and also ask them for help when I need it.

—Sara, mom of two

Try to take part in their culture and traditions.

—Yvonne, mom of two

Practicum

* How has your relationship with your mom changed since you became a mom?
* Some ways my extended family shows their love are . . .
* Ways I can connect my child with our extended family are . . .

3.3.3 Unsafe Relationships

As moms, engaging multiple people in healthy relationships creates a supportive circle for our family. However, not all relationships are healthy or even safe. When it comes to the two inner rings of relationship, it's just as important to know who to keep out as it is who to allow in. No one is perfect, and if they make mistakes we need to forgive in the same way we need them to forgive us. But if a person in your life consistently displays unsafe or unhealthy behavior and repeatedly resists change, strongly consider keeping them at the outside parameter of your circle of relationships. (If the unsafe relationship is a family member or even your husband, consider seeking professional advice on how to handle the relationship.) Dr. Henry Cloud and Dr. John Townsend suggest that unsafe people tend to display certain character traits. Proceed with caution if any of the people in your middle or inner circle consistently display the following traits:[11]

1. Think they "have it all together" instead of admitting their weaknesses
2. Are religious instead of spiritual
3. Are defensive instead of open to feedback
4. Are self-righteous instead of humble
5. Apologize but don't change their behavior
6. Avoid working on their problems instead of dealing with them
7. Demand trust instead of earning it
8. Believe they are perfect instead of admitting their faults
9. Blame others instead of taking responsibility
10. Lie instead of telling the truth

11. Are stagnant instead of growing
12. Avoid closeness instead of connecting
13. Are concerned about "I" instead of "we"
14. Resist freedom instead of encouraging it
15. Flatter us instead of confronting us
16. Condemn us instead of forgiving us
17. Stay in a parent/child role instead of relating as equals
18. Are unstable over time instead of consistent
19. Are a negative influence on us, rather than a positive one
20. Gossip instead of keeping secrets

 Practicum

* If you identified someone in your life who consistently displays unsafe traits, what steps do you need to take to ensure healthy relationships for yourself and your child?

* Do you recognize any of the traits listed in yourself? If so, how could you become a safer friend?

 Quick Review

Close friends and extended family provide a ring of support and caring.

- Becoming a mom changes our friendship needs.
- Friendships offer many benefits.
- Extended family relationships can be tricky but offer a rich resource of love for our kids.
- Proceed with caution if you discover someone with unsafe traits in your middle or inner circle.

3.4 Parenting Partners and Marriage: The Inner Circle

In the innermost circle of our relationships is the person moms regularly partner with to raise great kids. Historically this parenting partner has been a husband or the child's father, but with the growing number of single mothers, other adults are stepping into this role (according to the Center for Disease Control, 40 percent of children born in 2007 had a single mom). Having two parents is still optimal for a child's well-being, and later in this section we'll look at ways to invest in a healthy marriage. But research also shows that, whether married or single, a high-quality parenting partner makes shaping a healthy, resilient child easier.

3.4.1 Parenting Partner

The most likely parenting partner is your husband if you're married. If you're not married or have a spouse who isn't engaged with your child for some reason, the role can be filled by someone else you trust, can communicate with, and believe will provide a consistent presence in your child's life.

After a divorce or if you've never married, your child's father may serve as a parenting partner. A legal agreement on roles and responsibilities can help shape that relationship if needed. Other good options for a parenting partner include your mother, mother-in-law, or sister. While close relatives are more likely to be a consistent part of the child's life, you may also consider another single parent, a godparent, or a longtime friend.

A parenting partner relationship should provide practical support to fulfill the day-to-day responsibilities of caring for a child as well as emotional support such as a listening ear or a break when you're tired. Mental support is also important; a partner can help research things like day care options and health issues. Finally, a parenting partner can provide spiritual support, praying for your child and modeling a strong relationship with God.

Expert Take:
Parents who have a good relationship are more likely to:

- Feel successful as parents most of the time
- Experience fewer challenges as parents
- Actively seek support from immediate or extended family
- Feel confident in dealing with the daily challenges of parenting
- Consistently do many things that help their child grow up healthy[12]

FIELD STUDY

Help Is Only a Phone Call Away

Right out of high school I became pregnant. My mother understandably was somewhat ashamed, but eventually she came around and prepared me for labor. She was very instrumental in my early development as a young mom, having been one herself. I don't know what I would have done without her help.

When I first brought my daughter, Devoneé, home I had no idea what I was doing. I was a baby raising a baby. For example, when Devoneé was about a week old, I was changing her diaper and holding her on my lap. She was laughing and kicking around like naked babies do when suddenly I felt this warm liquid seep down my leg. "Gross," I hollered. My mom was sitting right next to me. "Take her, Mama," I said and practically tossed my baby into her arms. "That is so nasty."

"Janella, she just went potty, you put a diaper back on her," my mom said. But I had already dashed to the bathroom to dry off. I could hear my mother chuckling in the background. We still laugh about that today.

Another time, when Devoneé was two years old and I had moved away from my mother, I called her for advice. Because of some of the bad experiences I had when I was a child, one thing that was really hard for me was letting Devoneé out of my sight. But she wanted to do things by herself like run out to the mailbox and get the mail. This was nerve-wracking for me. I would stand there and watch her like a hawk to make sure no strange men were hanging around. I was driving myself crazy so I called my mom and asked her what I should do. I'll never forget her advice: "Janella, you know how when Devoneé was really little and she would hold tightly to your hand when you went for walks? Now that she's older, she's going to start wriggling her hand out of yours. She needs some freedom, you have to let go of her hand." I knew my mother was right. I've slowly been able to let go; it's not easy but I know it's necessary.

Over the years I've called my mother countless times to ask her questions about raising my baby girl. I've been so thankful that's she always only a phone call away.

—Janella, mom of one

Mom Stats

Who is your primary partner in parenting?

Child's father, my husband: 96.2%
Child's father, not my husband: 0.7%
My mother: 0.6%
Relative other than my mother: 0.3%
Friend: 0.7%
I don't have a parenting partner: 0.9%
Other: 0.6%

Mom Stats

What percentage of parenting responsibilities do you hold?

Less than half: 3%
More than half, but not all: 84%
Almost all: 13%

Practicum

* The biggest benefit of having a parenting partner is . . .
* I wish someone would help me with . . . M
* If you don't have a parenting partner, is there someone in your life you could ask?

3.4.2 Marriage

"If you want fifty years of marriage, forget about giving fifty-fifty. A lasting marriage requires that each partner give 100 percent." During their recent fiftieth anniversary celebration, this was the secret to marital success my parents shared with family and friends. I've had a front-row seat to their marriage, close enough to know they've experienced some tough stuff, gone through some bumpy patches, and—for better and for worse—I can verify they've practiced what they preach.

Research on marriage shows what a positive impact a healthy marriage has on children in a family. I realize that through my parents' marriage I've been given a priceless gift—a gift my husband and I are committed to giving to each other and to our own four children. Bucking the statistics, which indicate that one-third of adults who have been married have experienced at least one divorce,[13] means keeping our vows to each other. Sharing marriage vows took less than five minutes; keeping them is the work of a lifetime.

In his book *The Mystery of Marriage*, Mike Mason offers this thought-provoking take on courtship and marriage:

For in the first place, love convinces a couple that they are the greatest romance that has ever been, that no two people have ever loved as they do, and that they will sacrifice absolutely anything in order to be together. And then, marriage asks them to prove it.[14]

What happens to our vow, to giving 100 percent, when mothering consumes so much time? Becoming parents can bring more "better" than ever before, but it can also bring out the "worse." Quite honestly, the first three to six months after each of my children arrived was such a blur of fatigue, falling in love with baby, and figuring out how to meet the needs of my new little love, that it's hard to remember either the better or the worse.

Almost universally, moms coming out of the blur stage (I'm guessing dads, too, but I haven't been talking to them) note a definite shift in the relationship, often into something more practical and less intimate. There's the terrific—sitting at dinner together and watching in wonder as baby figures out how to pick up Cheerios with her little fingers. There's the tedious—picking up all the Cheerios that landed on the floor, along with cleaning the high chair and baby. And there's the terrible—feeling too tired after all that clean-up for bedtime to include anything but sleep. Note how terrific, tedious, and terrible all revolved around baby's needs?

It makes sense that we're focused on the practical side of meeting our kids' needs. They have a pretty endless list to be dealt with. But marriage needs more than caring for kids together to remain healthy (and romantic). Mom feeling touched-out and dad feeling untouched doesn't exactly promote romance. Mom feeling consumed by her new role and dad feeling left out is a recipe for disaster.

Disaster prevention is critical for your marriage and your child. Michelle Campbell, on staff with the Colorado Healthy Marriage Project, studies why marriage matters for our children and for the overall health of society. After extensive research, she offers the following comparison on children in a successful marriage versus those impacted by a failed marriage.[15] (The entire *Why Marriage Matters in America* brochure that lists all the impacts is available for free at www.marry-well.org.)

Marital Success	Marital Failure
Greater overall success in school	More likely to repeat a grade
Better reading abilities	Lower reading, spelling, and math scores
More likely to attend college	More likely to drop out of school
More likely to get high status job	Low confidence and self-esteem
More likely to marry	Difficulty with peer pressure relationships
Less likely to divorce when married	More and worse social problems

Other positive social impacts of a healthy marriage include better physical and mental health for both parents and kids, better parent-child relationships, less domestic violence and child abuse, and even longer life.

Research consensus is that not just any marriage, but a healthy marriage is optimal for a child's well-being. The best thing a married mom can do to shape a healthy, resilient child is to nurture her marriage. The Healthy Marriage Project believes there are three keys to a healthy marriage:

1. *Good communication.* Check out the Healthy Communication Rules Michelle shares in the sidebar on page 175. They can be used for discussing anything from discipline challenges to finances.

2. *Commitment to your relationship.* This includes making your marriage a priority, even over your child. Spend time together free of distractions. Translated: find reliable child care and plan regular date nights (consider biweekly or monthly).

3. *Love.* Ask questions about his day. Share what you appreciate about him. Look out for his best interests. Forgive. Keep the romance alive.

To those three keys, I would add two more:

4. *Maintain a sense of humor.* Laugh together and be willing to laugh at yourself.

5. *Pray for and with each other.* Invite God, the author of marriage, to guide, grow, and protect your relationship.

As moms, we can't control our husband's choices, but we can give our 100 percent to the relationship. If you are having difficulty with your marriage—especially if the difficulty includes abuse, addictions, abandonment, or adultery—seek help immediately from a pastor, professional counselor, or marriage workshops such as those offered by the Colorado Healthy Marriage Project.

Healthy Communication Rules

For the speaker:
- Speak for yourself.
- Keep statements brief.
- Stop to let the listener paraphrase.

For the listener:
- Listen without interrupting.
- Paraphrase what you hear.
- Focus on the speaker's message.

For both speaker and listener:
- Speaker always has the floor.
- Speaker shares the floor while listener paraphrases.

FIELD STUDY

Who Does What When Two Become Three or More?

Our friends, Susie and Chris, handed my husband, Frank, an envelope as we all relaxed in their living room. Our little guy, Tyler, who was only eight days old, slept peacefully, snuggled up in my arms, content with a full tummy. Frank opened up the envelope, which contained a comic strip, and started laughing.

"We thought of you two when we saw this," Susie mentioned.

Frank placed the comic on the coffee table so I could see it, too. It was a picture of a couple holding hands, looking into a crib, and telling a third person, "We decided to hire a sitter to do our jobs so we can stay home with the baby."

That was exactly what Frank and I wished we could do. We both had worked before we had Tyler and now both of us wanted to stay home. During my pregnancy, we had spent hours deciding what we were going to do and had come up with a plan to hold 1.5 jobs between the two of us. We also made a commitment to continually reevaluate and redefine our roles as needed.

Three children and sixteen years later, this method has worked pretty well for us, especially the continual reevaluating part because we have had to make changes when things were not going well. For instance, after our second child, Delaney, was born I took on a consulting job that was just too much. To keep my commitment I had to work long days. I would nurse Delaney at 4:30 a.m., catch a 6:20 a.m. train from San Diego into LA, work all day, and get home around 8 p.m.

One evening on my way home, while pumping breast milk in the small lavatory on the train, I realized my life was way out of balance. I felt totally disconnected from my family. *I hardly even know my own daughter,* I thought as I screwed the cap onto the full bottle, trying not to spill a drop as the train bumped along on the track. I knew I didn't want to keep up the pace this particular contract required. Within a week, I called the company and asked if I could do more at home and they agreed.

Over the years, Frank and I have swapped back and forth as needed on who worked what jobs and which of us stayed home more. Beyond just settling for an either/or approach to work and family, we have shared these roles through home-based work, part-time positions, and entrepreneuring new ventures. We've been able to make this work and our children have benefited by experiencing both parents' strengths along the way. My advice to couples trying to define their parenting roles is to not just buy others' ideas or rigid options about work style. Read everything you can find in the Bible about what makes a good spouse and parent, ask God who he has fashioned you to be, and pray for your husband to know his calling, too. Communicate about how your choices can best reflect the talents God gave you to invest in each other, your family, and your world.

—Naomi, mom of three

First Corinthians 13 is used as the Bible text during many marriage ceremonies, including mine. This poetic description of love illustrates the actions and attitudes of not only a healthy marriage, but every relationship within our circle.

Love never gives up.
Love cares more for others than for self.
Love doesn't want what it doesn't have.
Love doesn't strut,
Doesn't have a swelled head,
Doesn't force itself on others,
Isn't always "me first,"
Doesn't fly off the handle,

Doesn't keep score of the sins of others,
Doesn't revel when others grovel,
Takes pleasure in the flowering of truth,
Puts up with anything,
Trusts God always,
Always looks for the best,
Never looks back,
But keeps going to the end.

—1 Corinthians 13:4–8 Message

 ## Practicum

* Since you became a mom, describe one terrific, one tedious, and one terrible thing about your relationship with hubby.
* Of the five keys to a healthy marriage listed on pages 173–74, which one needs more of your focus? Ⓜ

Quick Review

A parenting partner is important in shaping a healthy, resilient child.

- A lasting marriage requires that each partner gives 100 percent.
- A successful marriage offers valuable benefits to our children and society.
- Communication, commitment, love, humor, and prayer are key to a healthy marriage.

At two o'clock in the morning, I am awakened by the appearance of a person no taller than a fire hydrant, only his black eyes visible over the horizons of the mattress.

"What do you want?" I whisper.

"Nothing," he whispers back . . .

His search for reassurance leads him to our bed, where two terribly fallible people toss and turn, the closest thing he knows to God.

—Anna Quindlen, *Living Out Loud*[1]

PART FOUR

GRANDSCAPE

grand (adj.): 1. large and impressive in size, scope, or extent; 2. main; of chief importance; 3. meriting the highest praise or regard

scape (noun): denoting a broad view or a representation of a view

grandscape (noun): the broadest view of life—those things seen and unseen; the past, present, and future; both cosmic and earthly, mortal and immortal, infinite and enduring for all time

4.1 Discovering Love in the Grandscape

4.1.1 Loves Me Like a Mom

FIELD STUDY

He Loves Me!

Before I became pregnant I didn't think about God. Or at least I tried not to. To me, God was a figure I learned about in Sunday school, but as I grew older he didn't fit into my everyday life. When my kids came (three in five years), my need grew. I needed God. NEEDED him. I couldn't make it through the day in my own strength. I didn't always know how to handle the role of being a mom. I needed so much more than I could provide for myself. When my kids sucked everything out of me God was faithful, filling me up again as I sought him.

I became a Christian when I was seventeen years old and pregnant. From that moment, I begged God to change me. I was a wild, self-seeking teen and I wanted to be more like Jesus. Very naïve, I prayed for love, joy, peace, and patience . . . but I had no idea that God had already set the process in motion. I had no idea that I'd be shaped in all those areas as a mom. Oh, don't I wish the shaping had been less painful, too! All that squishing, stretching, and smooshing hurts. Sometimes God met me when I was curled into a ball under my comforter, praying for help. He was there loving me when I had sick kids, lost kids, and disobedient kids. And, boy, am I glad.

—Tricia, mom of three

Like Tricia, when I became a mom I understood God's love in new ways. I realized he enjoyed being with me, just like I enjoyed being with my kids. God's desire to protect me was similar to my desire to protect my children. This reminds me of one of my favorite pieces of poetry, penned by an ancient writer named Isaiah.

> He tends his flock like a shepherd:
> He gathers the lambs in his arms
> and carries them close to his heart;
> he gently leads those that have young.
>
> —Isaiah 40:11

These words describe how God loves moms in much the same way we love our kids. God tends to moms, ensuring we're nourished and safe even as we tend our kids. God holds moms close to his heart while we're engaged in cuddling our little ones. God provides a place of comfort when we're cranky, scared, hurt, confused, or just need a little more attention. Ever found yourself in one of those places?

> Who has measured the waters in the hollow of his hand,
> or with the breadth of his hand marked off the heavens?
>
> —Isaiah 40:12

I did an experiment once to see how much water I could hold in the palm, or hollow, of my hand and it was less than two teaspoons. Compared to God's hand, which can hold all the waters of the earth, my two-teaspoon-sized hand seems insignificant. Does God really care about something so small?

Go outside and see how much of the sky you can measure off with one hand. Really, try it! Then, while you're out there, imagine the vastness of a hand that is large enough to span the entire heavens. The size of God's hands is inconceivable. God, whose hands shape and sustain the entire grandscape, extends those same hands to lovingly embrace, shape, and guide moms. The psalmist, David, poetically describes the intimate understanding and inescapable watch-care of God in Psalm 139. Consider how this poem compares with the way a child thinks of her mom.

O LORD, you have searched me and you know me.	My mom's constantly thinking about me.
You know when I sit and when I rise; you perceive my thoughts from afar.	She organizes all the stuff I do and cares about what's going on in my life.
You discern my going out and my lying down; you are familiar with all my ways.	She always knows what I'm doing; I think she has eyes in the back of her head!
Before a word is on my tongue you know it completely, O LORD.	She figures out what I want, sometimes even before I do. It's kind of weird, actually.
You hem me in—behind and before; you have laid your hand upon me.	She's always trying to protect me, holding my hand when danger is near.
Such knowledge is too wonderful for me, too lofty for me to attain.	She knows my favorite food, can find my missing shoe, and keeps a supply of snacks, Band-Aids, and toys in her purse. How does she know me so well?

Where can I go from your Spirit?
Where can I flee from your presence?
If I go up to the heavens, you are there;
if I make my bed in the depths, you are there.

I know she'll come find me, even
if I rocket to the stars or dig to the
center of the earth.

If I rise on the wings of the dawn,
if I settle on the far side of the sea, even there
your hand will guide me,
your right hand will hold me fast.

She's there for me when I wake
up in the morning, as I fall asleep
each night, and every minute in
between.

—Psalm 139:1–10

I didn't even come close to fathoming the concept of God's kind of love until I'd been a mom for a while. My children, amazing as they each are, at times wound me when they show indifference to my love or disregard my instruction. They try my love in a thousand different ways, fussing for hours with no apparent reason, whining about something as trivial as a broken cookie, slinging barbed words that sting my soul, slamming doors when I try to reconnect, breaching my trust in areas I thought were secure. I may not like them much at those times, but I do love them. That's the way God loves me. That's the way God loves you.

I have loved you with an everlasting love;
I have drawn you with loving-kindness.
—Jeremiah 31:3

 Practicum

* What do I think of a God who loves me like that?
* What do I think about this idea that God welcomes and celebrates a relationship with me?

4.1.2 What Kind of Love?

In a survey of 1,200 moms, 97 percent believed in God, 1 percent did not believe in God, and 2 percent said they weren't sure. Of the moms who believed in God, descriptions of God varied. Here are a few.

VOICES

I view God as. . .

Loving, caring, and all-powerful.

—Joann, mom of three

Something bigger and more complex than I'll ever be able to comprehend.

—Marne, mom of one

As someone that doesn't mean to play games with your life but he does.

—Wendi, mom of two

Someone whose love is big enough to let me come screaming and kicking in rage to his arms, as well as to let me curl up for comfort or even just companionship. Someone who loves me and wants me to be his no matter what I've done or how I've messed up.

—Tally, mom of four

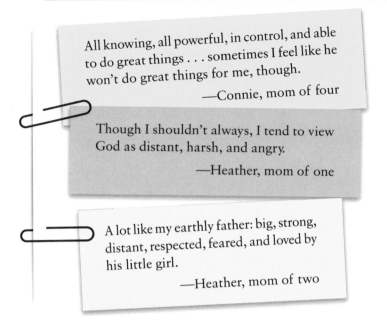

All knowing, all powerful, in control, and able to do great things . . . sometimes I feel like he won't do great things for me, though.

—Connie, mom of four

Though I shouldn't always, I tend to view God as distant, harsh, and angry.

—Heather, mom of one

A lot like my earthly father: big, strong, distant, respected, feared, and loved by his little girl.

—Heather, mom of two

How is it that moms—and people in general—hold so many different views of God? Could it be because we define God based on personal experiences?

Immersed in learning about God my entire life (I started attending church at the ripe old age of one week!), I've occasionally found myself defining God by my experiences. The most memorable occurrence was after my second miscarriage. My pregnancy ended a few days before Mother's Day and a few days after one of my junior high students announced she was having her second child. Her first was already in foster care. During that painful time, I defined God as a capricious entity, careless about life in general and my feelings in particular. I couldn't see beyond my own reality. Now I see how God was there for me, but at the time it felt like he just didn't care.

At times we also attempt to define God by the suffering and pain in the world around us. When asked to complete the statement "God really makes me mad when . . . ," moms responded—

I look at my son with autism and I think, *Why him?*

—Traer, mom of three

He doesn't email me his plan for my life. ☺

—Kristina, mom of three

People die from things we have no control over—floods, hurricanes, heat, etc.

—Cosette, mom of two

I can't understand his justice system. When I can't reconcile "why" he lets things like child slavery and starvation around the world continue to exist.

—Darcy, mom of three

A six-year-old sexually molested by a neighborhood friend, fathers deserting their children, city blocks incinerated by a bomb delivered in the name of god—examples of our pain-filled world are legion. It's not surprising some of us get mad at God, defining him as disengaged and uncaring. Philip Yancey addresses the question of where God is in painful situations with this statement: "He is in us—not in the things that hurt—helping to transform bad into good. We can safely say that God can bring good out of evil; we cannot say that God brings about the evil in hopes of producing good."[2]

I think the original description of the grandscape, found in the first book of the Bible, Genesis, supports Yancey's statement. God created a perfect, pain-free world, but humankind chose to push past God's safety barriers, bringing pain and suffering into the grandscape. Think about how you prepared your home for your little ones—plugging outlets, gating stairs, locking away poisons, even adding an annoying safety lock to the toilet. And yet, our clever kids figure out a way to get around those barriers to get what, and where, they want. During naptime, my youngest once pulled out his dresser drawers to create a stairway to the window, pushed out a secured screen to reach the backyard, stacked a little table and chair to access the gate latch, and made his way to his desired goal—the street. I worked hard to create a safe environment for my son, but he made choices that pushed beyond what I said was safe.

Perhaps you've made a similar choice at one time or another? When our desires push against God's safety barriers, we often bring additional pain into the world, to ourselves, and to others. When other people ignore God's safety barriers, they also bring pain into our world. And sometimes that pain leaches into countless lives. God didn't create an evil, pain-filled world anymore than I created a path to the street for my toddler. But, as Yancey states, "God does bring good out of evil."[3]

When my son returned home (hand-in-hand with an indignant neighbor who accused me of being a careless mom) I used the opportunity to teach him more about safety. Although there were consequences for his dangerous choice, I also gratefully and lovingly embraced him, thankful he was safely home.

In her book *The Girl in the Orange Dress*, Margot Starbuck chronicles her journey in understanding God as she comes to terms with her experiences of losing and gaining and losing fathers through adoption and divorce.[4] Near the end of her book, Starbuck tells about a time when a teacher shared about Jesus's parables of lost things—coins and sheep and sons. She writes, "I began to hear Jesus saying, 'I want you to know what my Dad is like.'" A few paragraphs later she continues, "He [Jesus] wanted each sheep and coin, son and daughter, to know that however we have found ourselves lost—to sin or shame, to guilt or depression, to despair or death—the Father longs for us to come home and to discover what he's really like, finding ourselves in the picture of his love." Starbuck discovered she couldn't define God based on her experiences with her earthly fathers—whether adoptive fathers, stepfathers, or especially her birth father who rebuffed attempts at relationship. Starbuck discovered that, unlike her birth father, God did not want her to remain lost.

"Quick! Bring the finest robe in the house and put it on him. Get a ring for his finger and sandals for his feet. And kill the calf we have been fattening. We must celebrate with a feast, for this son of mine was dead and has now returned to life. He was lost, but now he is found." So the party began.

—Luke 15:22–24 NLT

FIELD STUDY

God in the Midst of Pain

Something's wrong, he's not latching on, I thought as I tried to nurse Jake. I wanted to believe what the doctor was telling me. Jake wasn't quite ready to start nursing because of the intense thirty-minute labor and delivery. As a pediatric nurse I knew this was common, but I had this uneasy feeling.

Finally, after twelve hours, Jake latched on but he kept coughing and spitting up. *Something's really wrong . . .* I tried to squelch that nagging feeling. The nurse was in my hospital room conducting the discharge assessment. *Everything's fine, I'm just tired,* I tried to reassure myself.

"Well, everything looks good. Are you ready to go home?" the nurse asked.

"Yeah," I paused, "except Jake hasn't been eating well. It seems like he can't swallow."

"Let me watch you nurse him," she suggested, so I tried to feed him and he started coughing and spitting. Immediately concerned, she made some calls.

Soon a growing number of doctors and nurses were in my room. I knew this wasn't a good sign.

Home caring for our other children, my husband didn't answer my call, so I was relieved when my sister walked into my room. She's one of my best friends in the whole world. It seemed to me like God had sent her at just the right moment.

After two hours, the doctor came in and told me what I didn't want to hear.

"Jake needs emergency surgery. His esophagus is not connected to his stomach. Instead, his trachea is connected to his stomach and that's why he can't keep anything down. We need to operate to fix it. This is a serious condition and can be life threatening."

His words echoed in my head: *life threatening, surgery, trachea connected to his stomach.* I needed my husband. Finally, my sister reached him and he joined me at the hospital.

When they wheeled Jake into the room to spend the night with us, he had tubes coming out all over him and bandages on the spots where they drew blood, and he looked so tiny and frail. We held him all night long, wondering if this would be our only night.

Around 1:00 a.m., Steve came across Psalm 46: "God is our refuge and strength, an ever-present help in trouble. Therefore we will not fear . . ."

Lord I'm so scared, I prayed silently as Steve continued to read. "The LORD Almighty is with us; the God of Jacob is our fortress." We clung to those words throughout the night and during Jake's three-hour surgery the next morning.

To our relief, the surgery was successful. I wish this was the end of Jake's story, but one year later we're still dealing with complications. I've found I can't get through a single day if I don't draw on God for strength through reading the Bible and praying for our day. I would never wish this on anybody, but I've seen God even in the pain.

—Cindy, mom of three

Practicum

* I view God as . . .
* My view of God is formed by . . .

4.1.3 Loves Me as His Own

Defining God based solely on personal experience or bad events is like defining the world based on what we can see in our own backyard or even from a mountaintop. The grandscape is so much more than the landscape, and the Creator of the grandscape is so much more than our human experience. Once we invite God to break through our experience-based perceptions, we can begin to see the truth of who he is and how much he loves us. Because God is so much more than we are (remember the size of his hands!), knowing him is a lifelong journey that not only deepens our understanding of God but guides us in discovering our unique place in the grandscape. Wise King Solomon received this piece of advice:

> If you seek him, he'll make sure you find him. . . . Be brave, determined! And do it!
>
> —1 Chronicles 28:9 Message

Have you ever tried to make it easier for your child to understand more of who you are? My kids had a hard time comprehending that I was once a kid, so I showed them my baby pictures and grainy home movies. They don't understand what I do at work, so sometimes I take them to work with me, even give them opportunities to volunteer. They don't always pick up on how much I love their dad either, so I talk about our courting days and make sure they hear me tell Bruce "I love you" and see me kiss him hello and good-bye.

God did the same thing for us through Jesus. Jesus is God incarnate—God in the flesh, God with us. During his life on earth, Jesus was the picture of what it looked like to live as we were originally created to live, in the image of God. Jesus did God's work on earth and invited people to participate in that work. He healed the disabled, fed the multitudes, provided drinks for the thirsty, loved people of all sorts, and lived out God's purpose for his time on earth. Jesus also shared God's greatest "I love you" through his death and resurrection.

Why would Jesus do that? Why would Jesus even need to do that? The answer to the first question is that Jesus, who is fully God, loves us and wants to be in relationship with us, both in our present lives and in eternity. The answer to the second question is that on our own, we inherently push against God's boundaries for living. Our desire to "have things my way" separates us from God. The Bible calls that innate desire *sin* and tells us the penalty for sin is eternal separation from God. But God doesn't want to be eternally separated from you. He wants to be found. He wants an ongoing, loving relationship with you.

This is love: not that we loved God, but that he loved us and sent his Son [Jesus] as an atoning sacrifice [satisfactory payment] for our sins.

—1 John 4:10

Yet to all who received him [Jesus], to those who believed in his name, he gave the right to become children of God.

—John 1:12

Finding your place in the grandscape begins with accepting Jesus's gift of eternal relationship with God and believing that through him you are a child of God. If you haven't ever considered this before, I encourage you to talk to God about it today. Like a mom waiting to see her child after some time apart, he's eager to give you a big hug and chat for a while.

For God so loved the world that he gave his one and only Son, that whoever believes in him shall not perish but have eternal life.

—John 3:16

 ## Practicum

* How does being a mom who loves and would do anything for a strong, healthy relationship with her kids compare with how much God loves you and wants a healthy relationship with you?
* List some of the things that stand between you and accepting God's love . . .
* If you have unanswered questions, share them with other moms at mom-ology.org, or contact a Christian friend or a spiritual leader at a local church. M

Quick Review

God created the grandscape as a place to love people.

- God loves us like a mom.
- God's love is much bigger than a mom's love.
- God's love brings good out of bad things.
- God longs to be a part of our lives.

4.2 Discovering Purpose in the Grandscape

4.2.1 He's Number One

As a mom daily shaping your kids' future, you're already fulfilling an important purpose in the grandscape. Before your child was born, even before you were born, God designed you to be the mother your child needs, to love your child in a way that only you can love. Being a mom is one of the most important purposes of your life. It's not first though. In his best-selling book *The Purpose Driven Life*, Rick Warren explains our primary purpose:

> Bringing enjoyment to God, living for his pleasure, is the first purpose of your life. When you fully understand this truth, you will never again have a problem with

Mom Stats

I believe God has created me for a purpose.

Yes: 96.5%
No: 3.5%

Mom Stats

I know my God-given purpose in life.

Yes: 71.4%
No: 28.6%

feeling insignificant. It proves your worth. If you are that important to God, and he considers you valuable enough to keep with him for eternity, what greater significance could you have?[5]

Becoming a mom changed the way I spent my time, energy, and money. I willingly reordered my priorities around a seven-pounds-three-ounces little being. Often I even set aside or delayed things I once considered very high priority—such as washing my hair first thing in the morning—to be available for my baby daughter. For most moms, this is a lifelong change. I'm still a high priority with my mom, although now she does have time to wash her hair in the morning! When I moved to Colorado as an adult, my mom found a way to live here part of the time. When I needed surgery, she rearranged her life to take care of me and my family while I recovered.

Fulfilling our primary purpose of bringing enjoyment to God and living for his purpose involves a similar lifelong reorder. The more we make God our top priority, the more we'll understand who we are and what we were created to do. God's Word tells us, "It's in Christ that we find out who we are and what we are living for. Long before we first heard of Christ and got our hopes up, he had his eye on us, had designs on us for glorious living, part of the overall purpose he is working out in everything and everyone" (Eph. 1:11 Message).

Writer C. S. Lewis puts it this way: "The more we let God take us over, the more truly ourselves we become—because he made us. He invented all the different people that you and I were intended to be. . . . It is when I turn to Christ, when I give up myself to His personality, that I first begin to have a real personality of my own."[6]

Love the Lord your God with all your heart and with all your soul and with all your mind and with all your strength.

—Mark 12:30

 Practicum

* What does it look like to love God with all your heart?
* With all your soul?
* With all your mind?
* With all your strength?

4.2.2 Others Come Next

Immediately after stating our primary purpose for life, Jesus also establishes a secondary purpose: "Love others as well as you love yourself" (Mark 12:31 Message). If you're married, loving others as well as you love yourself includes loving your man. Likely, you vowed before God to do that. As a mom, loving others as well as you love yourself includes loving your child.

When it comes to loving those beyond our families, Jesus swings the door wide open in the parable of the Good Samaritan, found in Luke 10:25–37. In this parable, a Hebrew traveler is attacked and left for dead by the side of the road. Two religious leaders, also Hebrews, see the man, avert their eyes, and pass by without a word. A third man responds differently, even though he's from another culture. When he sees the man's condition, he demonstrates love in a very practical way, offering first aid, disinfecting and bandaging the traveler's wounds, and then lodging him at an inn to facilitate a complete recovery. Which of the men loved others? The one who responded to the need.

So our secondary calling to love others extends beyond the walls of our own families, beyond our circle of close friends, possibly even beyond our own culture and comfort zone. But with 6.7 billion people in the world, we can't show love to everyone. After your family and close friends, how do you decide which others to love?

God has gifted each of us with unique passions, hopes, abilities, interests, experiences, personality, and sphere of influence. Even during these hectic years of early mothering, he has placed you in specific situations where you can use your unique set of gifts to love others. If you're interested in discovering who else God is calling you to love, consider these ideas:

- *Get involved!* Look for opportunities to love others. Serve snacks to the hungry neighbor kids, volunteer to teach someone to read, befriend the teen mom in the condo next door. Consider each experience and what you learned about yourself through it. When you discover something that makes your heart sing, you've likely discovered who else you're called to love.

- *Value small.* Mother Teresa said, "I don't do big things, I do small things with big love." Great love is often disguised in small acts of kindness. Jesus modeled this by washing feet, spending time with children, fixing breakfast for friends, and going to dinner with an outsider.

- *Fear not.* Sometimes God calls us to love others in ways that seem beyond our capabilities. In ways that seem crazy for a mom with young kids. That's when it's especially important to follow through with the next two ideas: seek guidance from a trusted source and most importantly, ask God.

- *Seek guidance.* Ask a close friend, family member, or mentor to consider your gifts and situation and then share who they think you might consider loving.

- *Ask God.* He designed you to love others. Always. Consider asking him at the top of each morning, "Who are you calling me to love today?"

FIELD STUDY

Why I Said "Yes"

"We're looking for a woman to direct our women's ministry next year," our pastor announced. I felt this odd little warmth deep inside my belly and I found myself thinking, *I would so love to do that.*

Before I had my two children, I was involved in leading women's groups. I loved being a part of other women's lives and creating an atmosphere where women are growing. But with a husband who traveled and two small children, I had not plugged into a women's group much less led one, because I felt I didn't have the time. I didn't see how I could do it well at this stage in my life.

But I couldn't ignore the warmth in my belly; it really excited me to think about taking on this role. Then my friend Amy leaned over and said, "Suzie, you would be so good at that."

"I know, I totally want to do it," I blurted out, much to my own surprise.

I went home and wrote down all the reasons why I couldn't do it, most of them based on what I wanted to do with the little extra time I would have next year with the kids in preschool—two extra hours a day.

1. I want to sit down in peace and quiet and read a book in my rocking chair on my back porch.
2. I can't wait to clean out my closets.
3. I want to organize my laundry room.

The list continued. Then I stopped and reread what I had written. I thought, *Well, that's dumb. I can definitely put those things off to do what I know I'll enjoy doing.*

I realized I could do this, but I would have to do it differently than the previous woman who had directed the group. For one thing, I knew I couldn't do it alone. I invited five other women to join me and they all agreed.

I stepped into a new role that filled a passion I have always had, a passion to help women grow. I have no regrets. I've also found I can still find time to sit on my porch in my rocking chair and read a good book every once in awhile.

—Suzie, mom of two

Practicum

* In the last few weeks, the people I have shown love to are . . .

* Someone whom God is calling me to show love to is . . .

* My heart sang after showing love to . . .

 Quick Review

God created you to live in the grandscape with purpose.

* Our primary purpose is to love God wholeheartedly.
* Our secondary purpose is to love others as well as we love ourselves.

4.3 Finding Him in the Grandscape

4.3.1 Making Space for Relationship

I have to admit, fulfilling my calling as a young mom makes it challenging to fulfill my primary purpose. With kids demanding my constant attention, it's tough to make time for God. In our survey, moms found an average of 5.9 hours each week to spend with God. In that same survey, 15 percent of moms responded to the question of how much time they spent with God by saying, "Not enough." Hmmm, doesn't seem like I'm the only mom struggling to find enough time with God.

As a busy seventeenth-century monastery cook, Brother Lawrence also faced the challenge of making enough space in his life for God. He addressed that challenge in a way I think works for busy moms: he tried to love God in whatever he did. Brother Lawrence felt that the key to friendship with God was not changing what you do but changing your attitude toward what you do.

What's that look like for a mom? As a brand-new mom, I tried to talk with God before my feet hit the ground each morning, then continued the prayer as I attended to a soggy diaper. I read my Bible during naptime and sang songs about God while I did the dishes and ran errands. I also took my children to worship services each week. Sounds great. And it was. For a while. But then the demands of mothering overwhelmed me and I gave up. It felt too hard to think of God's presence when my children were ever-present. Bedtime came later and morning wake-up time came earlier. Naptime was filled with laundry and phone calls and sometimes a very necessary nap for me! Then naptime disappeared altogether. I'd miss church because my oldest had a cold. The next week she gave it to her sister, so I'd stay home with another runny-nosed kid. By the third week, it was my turn to be sick. I made it to church about one out of every four Sundays.

One day, I shared with an older friend that I couldn't wait until my kids were bigger so I would have time for my relationship with God. She kindly told me that I would never have time if I didn't find time. She challenged me to rethink my situation more creatively and figure something out. She also prayed for me and followed up with me to see how I was doing with this.

I tried praying in the morning again, often pulling a child or two into bed to pray with me. I placed a box of tiny cards printed with Bible verses next to my kitchen sink to read while tossing a salad or wiping the countertops. I made it a point to thank God for his creation as I pushed the stroller along neighborhood sidewalks, and I began praying for my kids while I turned their dirty socks right-side-out. It didn't always feel like these were holy moments, but the more I incorporated spending time with God into my routine, the more time I wanted to spend with him. He faithfully met me as I gave him some attention throughout each kid-filled day.

In the *Spiritual Disciplines Handbook*, Adele Ahlberg Calhoun provides these encouraging words to moms: "Bonding with God is not an all-or-nothing endeavor. Some of us feel that if we can't give God a good uninterrupted half hour, we aren't giving him anything. Intentional time set aside for bonding is one of the best gifts we give anyone. But even small moments spent with God (or others) matter and eventually add up."[7]

Discovering more about God is becoming increasingly important in our culture. According to a 2009 Barna study, 88 percent of American adults say that "my religious faith is very important in my life."[8] Another 2009 Barna study revealed that as people understand more about religious faith, they are likely to place more emphasis on spiritual disciplines or practices that support a growing faith and deeper relationship with God.[9]

Some spiritual disciplines are well known. Prayer and Bible study came up most frequently in our mom survey, and keeping the Sabbath is another important one. Let's look at some ways moms can incorporate these spiritual disciplines into the routines of motherhood.

PRAYER

Breath Prayers. These short prayers, repeated throughout the day, remind us that God is the oxygen of our souls. Every breath is a gift of God and as we breathe a prayer, we offer that gift back to God. Inhale deeply, repeating a name for God. As you exhale, voice a deep desire of your heart. One example, commonly known as the Jesus Prayer, goes like this:

> Inhale deeply with, "Lord Jesus Christ."
> Exhale slowly with, "Have mercy on me."

A mom concerned about her child struggling to adapt to day care or a new school experience might offer this breath prayer:

> Inhale with, "Jesus, Shepherd."
> Exhale with, "Care for my child today."

Praying Scripture. Praying Scripture invites God to shape life with his Word. Over the years, I have frequently prayed Mark 12:30 for my children. "Father God, teach Danielle (or Natalie, Dillon, or Brittany) to love you with all her heart and with all her soul and with all her mind and with all her strength."

Try inserting your child's name into Psalm 139:13–14.

> For you created _____'s inmost being;
> You knit _____ together in my womb.
> Teach _____ to praise you because he/she is fear-
>   fully and wonderfully made;
> Your works are wonderful.
> Teach _____ to know that full well.

Prayer Partners. Some people pray best in community. Praying with another person or small group of people can provide greater focus, encouragement, and accountability to pray regularly. At a memorial service for a young mom friend, I listened as her prayer partner shared intimately about my friend's heart. Prayer had clearly drawn them together, strengthening each woman's faith as they walked together through the valley of death. Prayer partners can meet in person, over the phone, or online. By participating in a Moms in Touch group, I was able to partner with several other moms in praying for my children and their schools. (Find out more about Moms in Touch at www.momsintouch.org.)

BIBLE STUDY

Daily Engagement. Engaging with the Bible on a daily basis reveals who God is, who we are, and what he purposes for our lives. Some ways young moms find to engage daily include:

- *By phone.* Visit www.411god.net to receive a daily, one-minute Bible reading on your phone at the time of your choice.
- *By iPod.* Access a three- to six-minute portion of the New Testament. Designed so that in one year you can complete the entire New Testament. Click on www.godsipod.com.
- *In print.* Read a chapter a day directly from the Bible in book form (novel concept, I know), or download a portion of Scripture to read throughout the day at www.biblegateway .com. Select key words and you can find passages on specific topics.

Memorization. Colossians 3:16 invites us to "Let the word of Christ dwell in you richly." My friend Kari prints the verses she's memorizing on large index cards. Once she's memorized a verse, she adds it to a ring of cards for regular review. Regularly reviewing the verses you've memorized is key for long-term memory. How can moms import verses into already crowded brains?

- *Card in the car.* Many moms spend part of each day in the car. Print a verse on an index card and review it at stop lights. This is safer than text messaging, but do keep your eyes on the road!
- *Scripture in song.* Insert a CD filled with Scripture set to music. Google "Scripture in song" to find music that suits your taste. This is also a great way to occupy kids in the car.
- *Friendly competition.* I'm a bit competitive, so when my pastor challenged our Bible study group to memorize a chapter of the Bible, I dug in to finish first. Sad, I know, but often a bit of friendly competition gets the job done. Invite a friend to memorize with you, agreeing that whoever says it right first, treats the other to a few hours of free child care. Very motivating!

Dig Deep. Join a neighborhood or church Bible study with a teacher who encourages exploring a particular book of the Bible or biblical topic in-depth. Or make the most of naptime and try a free or low-cost seminary level Bible course online through ChristianCourses.com.

SABBATH

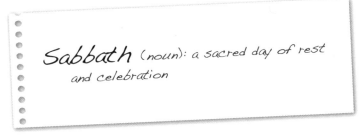

Sabbath (noun): a sacred day of rest and celebration

A third spiritual discipline that often gets crowded out of our busy lives is keeping the Sabbath. I confess that this is one I've been working on—again. Graduations and anniversaries and writing and work and family and husband and keeping house and . . . well, let's just say that the frenzied pace of the other six days of the week took over day number seven, too. As an attempt to quiet my soul one Sabbath, I started reading Dan Allender's very appropriately titled book, *Sabbath*. Allender writes of Sabbath as an invitation to enter delight, a "holy time where we feast, play, dance, have sex, sing, pray, laugh, tell stories, read, paint, walk, and watch creation in its fullness." It is "a day to celebrate God's re-creative, redemptive love."[10] Until that moment, I held a different definition of Sabbath that involved sleeping in, attending church, family lunch out, perhaps another nap, and then catching up from the past week and preparing for the week to come (which, if I thought about it too long, made me feel guilty so I avoided thinking about it). Allender suggests three core premises for celebrating the Sabbath:

- The Sabbath is not merely a good idea; it is one of the Ten Commandments God provided to guide our lives. (You can find them in the Bible in Exodus 20:1–17.) Funny how we still consider some of the ten—such as lying, murder, and adultery—as wrong, but think nothing of forgetting to keep the Sabbath sacred. Maybe it's not so funny. Maybe it's part of the reason we struggle in our relationships with God and each other.
- The Sabbath is a day of delight, not merely a day of "do nots" or a twenty-four hour vacation.

- The Sabbath is a feast day that anticipates days of joy and delight in heaven.[11]

I'm engaging in a different sort of Sabbath now, one that takes a bit of planning ahead and an intentional focus on the delightful. I still enjoy attending church and time with family. Oh, and the nap! But I've replaced the catch-up time with enjoying the outdoors, reading something just for me (not research for a book or work project), baking, and (most important for me) time to just sit quietly and think. At the close of my Sabbath, I feel less like a hamster on a treadmill and more like a well-loved daughter of God. If your frenzied pace has crept into day seven, if you're feeling too weary to delight in the grandscape, remember the Sabbath and engage in a day of sacred delight.

 **FIELD STUDY**

Sabbath Rest

The aroma of sage and garlic roasted chicken filled our kitchen, the salad was ready to serve, the warm rolls were in a basket, and the homemade chocolate cake sat on the counter ready to be enjoyed after dinner. The flurry of activity to get ready was over. *Whatever didn't get done, oh well*, I thought as I lit the candles and felt the eager anticipation I had come to feel every Friday night since we had decided as a family to observe the Sabbath—to spend the next twenty-four hours being together and simply resting.

Because we've chosen to use some Jewish traditions to enhance our Christian experience, our Sabbath starts at sundown on Friday night. To begin, we gather at the table in the dining room. Before we eat dinner, Trey, my husband, recites a prayer and a blessing over each of our children. My eyes fill with tears every time as I see how much he loves them and how important this is to him. Then he blesses me and I do the same for him before enjoying a leisurely dinner.

After dinner we clear the table, but we don't do the dishes. We let them sit in the kitchen sink until Saturday after sundown. At first this drove me nuts, but now I'm used to it and I know the kitchen will get clean eventually. After dinner we read a passage from the Bible. We might discuss it for a while, or if no one has much to say then we go watch a movie or play a game.

On Saturday we eat a simple breakfast, such as bagels, go to church, and then usually go out for lunch. Saturday afternoon we play and purposefully do not do any chores. We don't do our laundry or yard work or any type of housework. However, we are not super-legalistic about observing all the rules of the Sabbath; for example, if our son Anthony has a lacrosse game on Saturday, he'll play and we'll cheer him on. The point for us is developing a mindset of rest, a defined time to enjoy God, family, and friends and take a break from work.

For dinner Saturday, we eat leftovers from our meal the night before. Once Saturday evening rolls around and our Sabbath rest ends, we've spent time together, time to know God, and time for much needed relaxation.

I have a newfound sense of peace that I am learning to carry into every day of my life.

—April, mom of three

Note: The website April and her family use to shape their Sabbath is www.jewfaq .org. April shares that these instructions are a guideline, not a set of regimented rules, for developing a Christian approach to celebrating the Sabbath that incorporates Jewish traditions.

Besides prayer, Bible study, and Sabbath, there are many disciplines that encourage a deeper relationship with God. There is no one-size-fits-all plan for orienting our lives to God, but spiritual disciplines are as important to the soul as healthy eating and regular exercise are to the body. Below are some to consider as you seek to make space to love God wholeheartedly. Consider learning more about them at mom-ology.org, where you'll find a description of each discipline as well as suggestions for how you might incorporate it into your life. If you're looking for further information about spiritual disciplines, I've found the *Spiritual Disciplines Handbook: Practices That Transform Us* by Adele Ahlberg Calhoun provides great descriptions and practical, easy-to-understand ideas to try.

- Worship
- Communion
- Confession
- Journaling
- Rest
- Simplicity
- Solitude
- Silence
- Service
- Submission
- Mentoring
- Accountability
- Sharing Jesus
- Meditation

- Stewardship
- Fasting
- Giving

I will refresh the weary and satisfy the faint.

—Jeremiah 31:25

VOICES

I discover more about God when I . . .

Quiet myself and journal my thoughts and feelings to him.

—Dannelle, mom of two

Take time to listen and watch for him in my daily life and in the lives of my family and friends.

—Alena, mom of three

Look at things through my kids' eyes. As adults we take simple things like grass and rain for granted. But they look at it as an adventure or the most beautiful thing they have ever seen.

—Kristi, mom of two

Read the Bible. Pray. Ask questions.

—Jen, mom of two

Practicum

* I can better incorporate God into my daily routine by . . .
* A Sabbath day for my family would look like . . .
* Invite a friend or mentor to hold you accountable to new spiritual disciplines.
* Share your ideas with other moms.

4.3.2 The Family Plan

VOICES

I want my kids to see God as . . .

Integral in their daily lives, not just an insurance policy or sugar daddy we go to when all else fails or when we attend church on Sunday.

—Erika, mom of two plus foster kids

A prayer away. A place to go with all their concerns and troubles.

—Melanie, mom of three

The source of love, who loves them so much he made a way for them to be his friend, who will take care of them and do great things through them.

—Kelley, mom of three

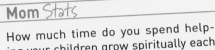

Mom Stats

How much time do you spend helping your children grow spiritually each
week?

As you deepen your relationship with God and uncover more about fulfilling your purpose in the grandscape, you'll likely want to engage your children in discovering God and his purpose for their lives. According to the Barna Group, that's important because a person's worldview is primarily shaped and is firmly in place by the time they reach the age of thirteen.[12]

Research reported in 2006 by The Heritage Foundation supports making spiritual development a priority. According to that study,

- Religious practice substantially benefits all aspects of life, especially family life. Marriages are happier; parent-child relationships are stronger; while domestic violence, divorce, and extramarital sex are all reduced.

- Students who regularly attend religious services enjoy significant gains in education, especially students from lower-income families.
- Religious practice is associated with improved overall physical and mental health.[13]

This doesn't mean that families engaged in developing a relationship with God through spiritual practices are immune from family challenges, but spiritual practices do reduce the risk.

While we can see the benefits of spiritual development, making it a priority for our families can be a challenge. Fewer than one in every five parents of young children believe they are doing a good job training their children morally and spiritually. As participants of another Barna study, parents who were asked to rank fifteen different performance indicators ranked their efforts related to morality and spirituality at the bottom of the list.[14]

Family Time Training, an organization whose mission is to train families to teach children Christian principles and values *in the home,* points out that the two most common reasons given for not providing spiritual training at home are "I'm too busy" and "Devotions are boring."[15]

I can relate to those responses. Although we had a few great family devotions at my house (my favorite utilized our dying grass to teach that while most things wither and die, God's Word remains forever), staying committed was tough when kids wiggled, fought, whined, and didn't seem to be learning much. Thankfully, organizations like Family Time Training offer free or low cost, quick, interactive ways to engage children in developing a relationship with God.

In reflecting on my early parenting years, I realized as my children became older, we spent less time learning about God together. I was very intentional about ensuring they had spiritual training (Christian school, church and Sunday school, listening to them pray before meals and at bedtime, biblically based media) and I prayed for them during my own prayer time each day. Those choices were good; however, I wish I would have engaged *with them* more often, praying for them at bedtime instead of just listening to their prayers, discussing spiritual concepts instead of sending them to Sunday school.

In Deuteronomy 6:5–9, God instructs parents to

> Love the LORD your God with all your heart and with all your soul and with all your strength. These commandments that I give you today are to be upon your hearts. Impress them on your children. Talk about them when you sit at home and when you walk along the road, when you lie down and when you get up. Tie them as symbols on your hands and bind them on your foreheads. Write them on the doorframes of your houses and on your gates.

How can we integrate spiritual development into daily family life? For ideas, take a look at the chart "Engaging Young Kids Spiritually." I've included practices that I did find time to incorporate as well as many I've gleaned from mom friends.

 Practicum

* Ask your child what he or she thinks about God. Ⓜ How can your family discover more about God together?

Engaging Young Kids Spiritually

Spiritual Discipline	Kid Engagement
Prayer	Make prayer for each other a part of meal and bedtime routine. Pray a Scripture promise or blessing over your child each day. Draw monthly family prayer partners. Pray for another family—keep a picture of the family on the fridge and locate them on a world map. Keep a family prayer journal. Pray together when you notice a need, for instance when a neighbor boy breaks his arm.
Bible Study	Share what you learn about God as you study the Bible. Read a Bible storybook together. Frame a favorite verse and place near your child's bed. "Read" it together every day. Act out Bible stories together. (For many years, my husband was a great donkey for Mary and Joseph as they looked for a room at the inn.) Make up songs to go with favorite Bible stories and sing them together.
Sabbath	Go for a nature walk and identify the prettiest, oddest, and most amazing things God made. Share about when you've seen God at work in the past week. Act out charades based on stories in a children's Bible storybook. Begin the Sabbath with a celebratory meal. Choose family favorites and include dessert. At least occasionally, attend worship services together as a family. While children's services can be fabulous, it is also good for our children to see us engaged in worship.
Fasting	Young children should not give up meals, but they can give up a favorite food for a period of time. This should be their decision, not yours! Go without a special treat for a while and give the money saved to help someone else.
Giving	Redeem recyclables and use the money to support a child in another country. Once they get past the "stick coins in my mouth" stage, give your child ten dimes each week and encourage them to give one dime back to God through the church offering. Have each family member give a favorite (and I don't mean old, worn-out favorite) piece of clothing, book, or toy to charity.
Serving	Pull weeds, plant flowers, or rake a neighbor's front yard. Make a meal together and deliver it to a new mom. Walk for a good cause. If your children are young, push them in the stroller or pull them in a wagon. Collect canned goods from neighbors for a local food bank. Visit a senior citizen's center and talk with the residents. Bring children's artwork to share.

4.3.3 A Faith Community

While parents hold the primary responsibility for the spiritual development of their children, a faith community can provide a support system of caring adults, friends, and activities that foster and reinforce spiritual values. A church offers families not only a community to worship with but prayer support, encouragement, spiritual teaching, and other resources that encourage a growing relationship with God.

If you're not currently involved in a faith community, consider using these ideas to find one that fits your family.

- Be prayerful. Allow God to guide the process.
- Remember, there is no perfect church!
- Decide what you're looking for.
  - » Church values and beliefs
  - » Size
  - » Location
  - » Type of service
  - » Opportunities to get involved
- Ask friends, family, neighbors for recommendations.
- Do a web search and visit possible church websites.
- Visit at least three times.
- Be patient. Finding a church can take time.

You are members of God's very own family, citizens of God's country, and you belong in God's household with every other Christian.

—Ephesians 2:19 TLB

FIELD STUDY

A Little Help from My Friends

I'm going to lose my mind, I thought as I watched my three-year-old son knock down yet another tower of Legos with his toy truck. Sitting on the floor of his room, I rested my back against his big-boy bed with my leg propped on a pillow. A few days earlier I'd fractured my knee in a skiing accident. The doctor ordered me to put no weight on my leg or risk the fracture splintering, which would require major surgery. Crutches were my new best friend.

Eight weeks, no problem, I thought, but after a few days I was feeling helpless and lonely. My husband, Zane, had to go back to work and I had told him not to worry; I would be a good girl and use my crutches. No hopping around the kitchen on my good leg like I had tried the day before, and no driving for the first few weeks.

I glanced at my watch. *It's only 10:30? This is going to be a looong day.*

Then I heard my ten-week-old baby cry.

"Uh oh, Josh," I said, "Jordan's awake." I grabbed my crutches and hobbled to his crib.

Then the doorbell rang. *What now?* I thought.

The tricky part was getting Jordan out of his crib and down the stairs. I had to carefully lift him out of his bed, balancing on my good leg, and then set him on my lap and scoot down the stairs step-by-step on my bottom. Josh carried my crutches for me. Once I reached the bottom stair, I scooted to the playpen and placed Jordan in it. Finally, I took my crutches from Josh and answered the door.

"Hi, thought you might need some help. I heard you broke your leg," the woman at the door said. She looked familiar but I didn't know her name. She was holding a casserole dish and a Ziploc baggie filled with salad. "I'm Jill, from Bible study. They made an announcement about your accident and we put together a schedule of meals for your family for the next few weeks. I brought you dinner for tonight."

"Wow, thanks," I replied. I had never had anyone do anything like this for me.

"I have some extra time, too. Can I help you with anything?" she asked.

"Oh no. I'm fine," I lied, wondering if she had seen me scooting around on my bottom.

"I could throw in a load of wash for you. I can't imagine how you could carry around a laundry basket," she smiled. Then we both started to laugh; she obviously had seen me. "Really, I'd love to do that. And we could sit and chat while it's running."

I humbled myself, accepted her help, and enjoyed her company.

She was the first of many women from my Bible study who came to help me. They brought meals, carried stuff up and down the stairs, took Josh to the park, took out the trash, vacuumed, and even scrubbed our bathrooms.

I was grateful beyond words for their personalized support through this tough time.

—Jean, mom of three

Mom Stats

Are you involved in a faith community?

Yes: 92%
No: 8%

VOICES

If you're not involved in a faith community, why not?

I have chosen not to be a member of the Christian community because I am not comfortable with how Christianity is being/has been used to justify specific positions.

—KS, mom of one

As a new mother, getting to church is sometimes not possible. Heck, getting a shower every day is not possible.

—Gavi, mom of one

I don't have the desire or time. I would like my daughter to have a bit of exposure to religion as she gets older.

—Dawn, mom of one

If you are involved, what is the best thing about your faith community?

My pastor has a real heart for people individually.

—Faith, mom of four

Being part of a close, intergenerational community that loves and cares for me and my children.

—Elizabeth, mom of two

Spiritual growth, deepening, and authenticity.

—Lydia, mom of two

My faith community is very "grace based." It's completely come-as-you-are with no judgment. We accept everyone and anyone regardless of circumstance and support them in their needs so they have a safe place to worship and develop or deepen their relationship with God.

—DeDe, mom of three

 Practicum

* When it comes to a faith community, I'm looking for a church that . . .

Quick Review

God wants us to get to know him better.

- We need to make space for our relationship with God.
- We can make space for God within the busy days of mothering through spiritual disciplines and sharing those disciplines with our children.
- Being part of a faith community supports spiritual growth.

4.4 Sharing Him in the Grandscape

4.4.1 Our Great Commission

Besides giving us the primary and secondary purposes of loving God and loving others, Jesus also gave us a commission. Digging into the Latin roots of the word *commission*, I discovered it means "together sent." Sent to what? Let's take a look at Matthew 28:19, also known as the Great Commission.

> Therefore go and make disciples of all nations, baptizing them in the name of the Father and of the Son and of the Holy Spirit, and teaching them to obey everything I have commanded you.

We, the friends of God, are together sent to share God with others—the people in our home, in our neighborhood, and beyond. Just as God extended his hand to you in friendship, he asks you to extend a hand of friendship to others. Just as God sent Jesus to help us understand him better, he sends each of us to help other people understand him better. God asks us to tell other people about the amazing, loving God who has become the most important part of our grandscape.

God commissioned us to work together so that as many people as possible will get to know him. We are together sent to share God and how to know him better with other people in the world.

There's also another aspect to "together sent," one I find very exciting. Once we have a relationship with God through Jesus, God's Spirit lives in us. When we share our lives with others, God is with us. We, along with God's Spirit, are together sent to share his love with others.

And surely I am with you always, to the very end of the age.

—Matthew 28:20

Our commission to share God with other people is most often carried out in three ways:

- Service to others
- Sharing our story
- Sharing God's story

All three of these flow out of our primary and secondary purposes, loving God and loving others.

Would a grandmother hide the pictures of her precious grand-baby from others? She loves them way too much to do that! Likewise, as you get to know God and allow his love to transform your life, you'll love him way too much to keep him a secret. Sometimes we think we have to wait until we've got a great story or had some supernatural experience with God before we share about him. Not really. God asks us to share our self and our story only in ways that reveal his love. When we extend our hand in love to other people, such as the moms and kids in our neighborhood or our co-workers, God is also extending his hand in love, and together we invite another person to find her purpose in the grandscape.

> So we have been sent to speak for Christ. It is as if God is calling to you through us.
>
> —2 Corinthians 5:20 NCV

FIELD STUDY
Serving Together

I pointed to India on the big flat atlas hanging on the wall of Adrian's room as I talked to my four-year-old about our upcoming trip to that country.

"What kinds of animals live in India?" he asked.

"Tigers, monkeys, camels, all kinds of different animals, but we might not see many animals because we're going to help the people who live there," I explained.

My sisters and my mom thought we were crazy to take our son on a trip with our church to visit the slums of India. Our purpose in going was to explore the possibility of partnering with another organization to help the Dalit people, also know as the "untouchables," who live in extreme poverty and oppression.

I guess because I had traveled so much before having kids, and my husband, James, and I are both committed to exposing our children to other cultures at an early age, we felt the opportunity for him to learn and to share God's love as a family outweighed the challenges of traveling with a preschooler.

Throughout our two-week visit, Adrian ran and played with the kids even though he couldn't speak their language. These are children who are treated as poorly as animals in that society, but he just saw them as kids like himself. He smiled and waved at the women who filled their water jugs each day from a well; women who are mostly ignored and are considered useless in their own country. He saw men and women who never received any form of education learn how to sew and lay bricks so they could earn a living.

I'm so glad we took Adrian with us, and we'll go again. From his point of view our worlds aren't so different. Most of all, he showed me how to share God's love with a childlike love, an innocent acceptance of others—the kind of love that makes a difference in the world.

—Rachael, mom of two

 Practicum

* I can serve others within my daily life by . . .
* The part of my life story that I could share to help another person understand how much God loves them is . . . [M]

4.4.2 Blessing for the Journey

When I became a mom, I experienced God's love in new ways. Being a mom also heightened my awareness that God created me for a purpose. That I, an ordinary mom, have unique significance and valuable purpose in the grandscape amazes me. God considers my contribution as a mom (and as a woman) an integral part of his magnificently ordered universe.

VOICES

My place in the universe is . . .

An epic adventure and planned by God.

—Heather, mom of four

To share God's love and message through everything I do, whether it's as a mom, wife, friend, etc. I admit I'm not always the best at this, but it's what I'm called to do.

—Jessica, mom of one

Heather and Jessica's understanding of their place in the grandscape reflects the eternal adventure God has planned for each of us. God's love for you is epic, a story you can and should tell others. God's love for you is heroic, as heroic as the love you daily, sacrificially lavish on your child. As you journey through the grandscape, I pray that you wholeheartedly discover God's love for you, that you love others like God loves you, and that you share the story of God's love with another person needing to find her place in the grandscape.

I'd like to share one final piece of poetry, a blessing, as you journey through the grandscape. Someday soon, pass it on to a sister traveler.

> May the LORD bless you
> and protect you.
> May the LORD smile on you
> and be gracious to you.
> May the LORD show you his favor
> and give you his peace.
>
> —Numbers 6:24–26 NLT

Practicum

* What do you think about your place in the universe?
* How is God blessing you in the journey?

Quick Review

God wants us to share his love with others as we journey through the grandscape.

- We are "together sent" to share God's love with the world.
- We share God through our service, our personal story, and God's story.
- As we share his love with others, God is with us.

CONCLUSION

SHAPING ME

Organizing the 1,800 individual survey responses for *Momology* started me thinking about how my mom shaped who I am today. Three biggies come to mind—her heart for kids to have great homes, her temper, and her integrity.

For me, having a mom who believes every kid deserves a great home meant having three foster siblings. Even as a young adult, the experience of losing my first foster sister generates a fear in starting new relationships. To let someone in is to risk losing them. On the positive side, two of my foster siblings are now my siblings through adoption. Watching that process and growing up in an adoptive family inspired my career choice—currently I'm in law school preparing to work in child and family law. I want to advocate for children in need of forever homes.

My mom's not perfect (from reading the survey responses I see that's pretty common). Taking care of four kids, her temper sometimes got the best of her—she likes to be in control. I inherited both tendencies. Watching my mom struggle to get a handle on her temper, having her apologize and continually work on this, has shaped me into a person who can face my own imperfections, apologize for my own mistakes, and offer second chances when others make mistakes.

I didn't always like the limits my mom placed on what I did. One of our biggest arguments ever was over seeing the movie *Titanic*; mom thought that steamy car scene at the end was inappropriate for a young teen. But she set those limits with integrity and stuck to them. We don't see eye-to-eye on every issue, but I always know where she stands. What she says matches how she lives. Her faith in God is like that, too. I think it's important to live what you believe.

—Britt, research assistant and daughter of author

It's great to have this feedback from my daughter, but I would've traded her college fund to have it when she was still a little girl! Wouldn't it be nice to have a magic mirror so we could ask every morning, "Mirror, mirror on the wall, what's the best decision of all?" With all the advances in technology, that capability still exists only in storybook land. Mothering is carried out in real life. We don't see the results until the bulk of our work is done.

In real life, moms are like scientists, researching and testing what we think our child needs to be a successful adult. But we're also artists, combining what we learn with a unique creativity and passion that influences the outcome of our child's life.

So we explore what it takes to raise a healthy, resilient child and we creatively incorporate those things into our mothering. We work toward building a healthy, resilient mom core. We develop finesse through daily living with our kids in a way we believe helps them become incredible big people. We interact in a circle of relationships that support and encourage us and our kids. We engage with God, seeking a deeper relationship with him and an understanding of our purpose in his grandscape.

But even with all that, most of us still worry, at least a little bit. Come on, haven't you ever asked yourself, "Am I doing it right? Am I ruining my child?" Moms can't see into the future, but God can. The last four lines of Psalm 139 guide us moms to take our worries to the everlasting Guide for shaping great kids.

> Search me, O God, and know my heart;
> Try me and know my anxious thoughts;
> And see if there be any hurtful way in me,
> And lead me in the everlasting way.
>
> vv. 23–24 NASB

ACKNOWLEDGMENTS

Carla, Jean, Alexandra, and Joy—more than an advisory team, you shaped *Momology* by sharing wisdom, ideas, research, personal stories, prayers, encouragement, and excellent first-look editorial input from your unique perspectives.

Janis—the hefty "Better Mom, Better World" research notebook you put together provided the foundation for *Momology*. Thanks for digging deeply and sharing freely.

Moms who shared their stories and survey participants—your personal stories bring to life the many different ways moms can shape themselves and their kids. Your survey responses were filled with thought-provoking and amusing comments. Thanks for taking time to share your mothering journey with us.

MOPS board, staff, field leaders, and volunteers—every day you invest in making better moms who make a better world. I'm thankful to be part of your circles. Liz, as always, I appreciate and value your theological expertise. Naomi, thanks for making space and prayerfully supporting me from beginning to end.

Elisa and Carol—during my own early mothering years, you constantly reminded me that God chose me to mother my kids. I hope *Momology* will provide that same message to this new generation of moms.

Andrea, Twila, and the team at Revell—you honed, expanded, illustrated, and clarified so many thoughts and ideas, taking *Momology* from a manuscript to an interactive exploration of mothering. You are wonderful to work with.

My family—thanks to Mom and Dad for shaping my foundation; Brittany, Natalie, Danielle, and Dillon for each uniquely and lovingly contributing to my mom education; and Bruce for faithfully partnering with me on our journey as parents. I love you who make up my innermost circle.

NOTES

Part One Core

1. *Promoting Healthy Families in Your Community*, Child Welfare Information Gateway 2008 Resource Packet, www.childwelfare.gov/pubs/res_packet_2008.

2. Ibid.

3. Donna Partow, *A Woman's Guide to Personality Types* (Grand Rapids: Bethany, 2002).

4. Lewis B. Smedes, *Shame and Grace: Healing the Shame We Don't Deserve* (New York: HarperCollins, 1993).

5. According to www.mayoclinic.com/health/forgiveness, accessed December 8, 2007.

6. Sherry Glied and Sharon Kofman, *Women and Mental Health: Issues for Health Reform* (New York: The Commonwealth Fund, 1995).

7. You can access this online album at the Postpartum Progress blog, http://postpartumprogress.typepad.com.

8. Amanda Gardner, "Mom's Depression Can Put Kids at Same Risk," *HealthDay News*, March 21, 2006.

9. Carrie Carter, "Women and Depression," www.mops.org/page.php?pageid=1987.

10. Tom Rath, *StrengthsFinder 2.0* (New York: Gallup Press, 2007), iii, 12. The book includes access to an online assessment. More information is also available at strengthsfinder.com.

11. Henry Cloud and John Townsend, *Boundaries: When to Say Yes, When to Say No to Take Control of Your Life* (Grand Rapids: Zondervan, 1992), 29-32.

12. Ibid., Part 2: "Boundary Conflicts."

13. K. Springthorpe, "Mama Burn Out," www.momblognetwork.com/content/mama-burn-out.

14. Katherine Ellison, *The Mommy Brain: How Motherhood Makes Us Smarter* (New York: Basic Books, 2005), chapter 2.

15. Og Mandino, *A Better Way to Live* (New York: Bantam, 1990), 96.

Part Two Finesse

1. YMCA and Search Institute, *Building Strong Families: A Preliminary Study on American Parents and Resources They Need to Succeed* (November 2002), 6. Accessed at http://www.search-institute.org/families.

2. Search Institute, *40 Developmental Assets for Early Childhood* (2005), accessed at www.search-institute.org/system/files/40AssetsEC.pdf.

3. Henry Cloud and John Townsend, *Raising Great Kids: Parenting with Grace and Truth* (Grand Rapids: Zondervan, 1999), 31–32.

4. Tim Kimmel, *Grace Based Parenting* (Nashville: W Publishing Group, 2004).

5. Josephson Institute, "Character Counts! Six Pillars of Character." For more information on this approach to character education, visit their website at http://charactercounts.org/sixpillars.html.

6. Harvey F. Silver and J. Robert Hanson, *My Decision-Making Style* (adapted for the Georgia Department of Education, 2003), accessed at http://my.ilstu.edu/~kawalst/DecisionMakingStyleInventory.pdf.

7. Brenda Hunter, *The Power of Mother Love* (Colorado Springs: Waterbrook, 1997), 1–3.

8. Dr. Seuss, *How the Grinch Stole Christmas* (New York: Random House, 1957).

9. *Promoting Healthy Families in Your Community.*

10. Ibid.

11. Cloud and Townsend, *Raising Great Kids*, 77–78.

12. David Elkind, PhD, *Ties That Stress* (Boston: President and Fellows of Harvard College, 1994).

13. William Sears, MD and Martha Sears, RN, *The Baby Planner* (Nashville: Thomas Nelson, 1994), 2.

14. "A Mother With Her Intuition . . . Will Know Just What to Do!" (personal blog), http://backtobasicskindofmom.blogspot.com/, posted May 15, 2009.

15. Martha Farrell Erickson and Enola G. Aird, *The Motherhood Study: Fresh Insights on Mothers' Attitudes and Concerns* (Institute for American Values, 2005), 8; available online at www.motherhoodproject.org.

16. From the March 2007 online publication *Discipline and Your Child* (American Academy of Pediatrics, 1998; updated January 2002), http://www.keepkidshealthy.com/cgi-bin/extlink.pl?l=http://www.aap.org/family/99disc.htm.

Part Three Circle

1. *Promoting Healthy Families in Your Community.*

2. Jolene Roehlkepartain, *Parenting Preschoolers with a Purpose: Caring for Your Kids and Yourself* (Minneapolis: Search Institute, 2006), 44.

3. *Building Strong Families.*

4. *Building Strong Families*, 3.

5. According to www.wickedlocal.com/Halifax, January 15, 2009.

6. Lisa Bergren, *Life on Planet Mom: A Down-to-Earth Guide to Your Changing Relationships* (Grand Rapids: Revell, 2009), 108.

7. Mollie Ziegler Hemingway, "White Flag in the Mommy Wars," *Christianity Today*, September 2009, 76.

8. Ibid.

9. Bergren, *Life on Planet Mom*, 101–2.

10. Karol Ladd and Terry Ann Kelly, *The Power of a Positive Friend* (West Monroe, LA: Howard Publishing, 2004), 59–60.

11. Henry Cloud and John Townsend, *Safe People: How to Find Relationships That Are Good for You and Avoid Those That Aren't* (Grand Rapids: Zondervan, 1996), chapters 2 and 3.

12. *Building Strong Families*, 4.

13. "New Marriage and Divorce Statistics Released," *The Barna Update*, March 31, 2008; accessed online at www.barna.org/barna-update/article/15-familykids/42-new-marriage-and-divorce-statistics-released.

14. Mike Mason, *The Mystery of Marriage: Meditations on the Miracle* (Colorado Springs: Multnomah, 2005), 53–54.

15. *Why Marriage Matters in America*, Healthy Marriage Project brochure. To download the entire brochure, visit www.marry-well.org or call 720-488-8888.

Part Four Grandscape

1. Anna Quindlen, *Living Out Loud* (New York: Random House, 1988).

2. Philip Yancey, *Where Is God When It Hurts?* (Grand Rapids: Zondervan, 1990), 109.

3. Ibid.

4. Margot Starbuck, *The Girl in the Orange Dress* (Downers Grove, IL: InterVarsity Press, 2009).

5. Rick Warren, *The Purpose Driven Life* (Grand Rapids: Zondervan, 2002), 64.

6. Quoted in Warren, *The Purpose Driven Life*, 80.

7. Adele Ahlberg Calhoun, *Spiritual Disciplines Handbook* (Downers Grove, IL: InterVarsity Press, 2005), 278.

8. "Americans Are Exploring New Ways of Experiencing God," *The Barna Update*, June 8, 2009, accessed at www.barna.org/barna-update/article/12-faithspirituality/270-americans-are-exploring-new-ways-of-experiencing-god.

9. "Many Churchgoers and Faith Leaders Struggle to Define Spiritual Maturity," *The Barna Update*, May 11, 2009, accessed at www.barna.org/component/content/article/36-homepage-main-promo/265-many-churchgoers-and-faith-leaders-struggle-to-define-spiritual-maturity.

10. Dan Allender, *Sabbath* (Nashville: Thomas Nelson, 2009), 5.

11. Ibid.

12. "Barna Survey Examines Changes in Worldview Among Christians over the Past 13 Years," *The Barna Update*, March 6, 2009, accessed at http://www.barna.org/barna-update/article/21-transformation/252-barna-survey-examines-changes-in-worldview-among-christians-over-the-past-13-years.

13. Patrick F. Fagan, *Why Religion Matters Even More: The Impact of Religious Practice on Social Stability* (The Heritage Foundation, December 18, 2006), accessed at http://www.heritage.org/Research/Religion/bg1992.cfm.

14. George Barna, *Revolutionary Parenting* (Carol Stream, IL: Tyndale, 2007), 10.

15. Check out the Family Time Training website at www.famtime.com.

Shelly Radic is Chief of Staff at MOPS International, author of *The Birthday Book*, and a regular contributor to MOPS publications. Her writing is informed by her education, mothering her four children, and twenty years of MOPS experience. She lives in Aurora, Colorado.

Following Jesus Shouldn't Be Just One More Thing to Do

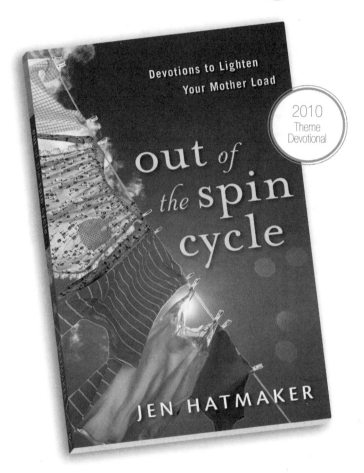

Jen Hatmaker delivers forty devotions based on the words and life of Jesus to provide relief for moms of all ages.

Revell
a division of Baker Publishing Group
www.RevellBooks.com